DREAM BRIDGE

MICT CHIB

МІСТ СНІВ

Вибрані вірші

Олег Лишега

З української переклали

Вірляна Ткач *та* Ванда Фіппс

ВИДАВНИЦТВО ЛОСТ ГОРС
Ліберті Лейк, Вашингтон

DREAM BRIDGE

Selected Poems
Oleh Lysheha

Translated from the Ukrainian by
Virlana Tkacz *and* Wanda Phipps

LOST HORSE PRESS
Liberty Lake, Washington

ACKNOWLEDGMENTS

The translators would like to thank Andrew Colteaux, Meredith Wright, Sean Eden, Chris Ignacio, Tom Lee, Andrew Pang, Olha Luchuk, Julian Kytasty, Olena Jennings, Svitlana Matviyenko, Waldemart Klyuzko, Ivan Malkovych, Oksana Lysheha, and Oksana Lebedivna. Special thanks to Ellen Stewart, the mama of La MaMa.

Series Editor: Grace Mahoney

Cover Art: Khystyna Kozyuk, *Delicate Bouquet,* oil on canvas, 38" × 33" Please visit Kozyuk Gallery online to view or purchase paintings: www.kozyukgallery.com.
Photo of Oleh Lysheha: Waldemart Klyuzko
Photo of Virlana Tkacz: Pavlo Terekhov
Photo of Wanda Phipps: Wanda Phipps
Book Design: Christine Lysnewycz Holbert

FIRST EDITION

This and other fine Lost Horse Press titles may be viewed on our website at www.losthorsepress.org.

LIBRARY OF CONGRESS CATALOGING-IN-PUBLICATION DATA
Cataloging-in-Publication Data may be obtained from the Library of Congress.
ISBN 978-1-7364323-7-2

LOST HORSE PRESS
CONTEMPORARY UKRAINIAN
POETRY SERIES

Volume Ten

ЗМІСТ

CONTENTS

Сон

Adamo et Diana

ВСТУП   INTRODUCTION

IT WAS AS FESTIVE INSIDE as it was cold, dank, and sleety outside. Virlana's apartment, as usual, in full force, after a performance of one of Yara's plays. Yara being the Ukrainian-USA theatre company in residence at La MaMa, off-off Broadway's Mecca. The footprints on the ceiling were almost gone, replaced by pogo stick dents and oar dips. In the back, someone was crying laughter, harmonizing with the room tone volcano ambience. The usual. The Hutsuls were bellowing. Mykola Riabchuk thought he was at Veselka and started ordering rainbows, etc. The etc. included Ihor Rymaruk— their Visimdesiatnyky (The Generation of the 1980s) anthology was being used as a menu! They were ordering Oksana Zabuzhko, Attila Mohylny and Victor Neborak (by now I was understanding Ukrainian) and, of course, the Mystery Man himself, author of this book you hold in your hand/is appearing on your screen, Oleh Lysheha.

I continued through the crow (I'm keeping this typo! I meant crowd of course). Bohdan Boychuk and Serhiy Proskurnia were doing breathing exercises (as if they were under water), the Korean-American accordionist, Susan Hwang, was playing while literally kicking up her heels. Julian Kytasty, representing Banduristan, and Virlana Tkacz herself, founder and director of the whole shebang, was dancing with her co-translator, Wanda Phipps, the mesmerizing poet, when word buzzed around, Lysheha has entered! More like an overcoat than a body. I tried to make my way towards the storied poet but was pushed back like a tide by the Hutsuls' horns which had started to bray at just that moment. There was a stomping, as if the room were filled with horses, and a hawk and a raven flew in (I might have been drunk) when, to my surprise, I found myself out on the sidewalk. It dawned on me that it was dawn, the next day. Cross bridge now, see Lysheha later.

Needless to say, it took a long time to be later. I can't say how long, but significantly I attended more parties at Virlana's, every party I could get to, and there must have been one or two every week, I couldn't tell who was living there even. You have to realize, this is a small East Village apartment we're talking about, and in the corner, a rabbit and a live fish, I don't know how. This was in the 90s, when Yara was doing a lot of Lysheha's poetry, turning it into plays, I have to remember that what I'm writing is an introduction to Oleh Lysheha's *Dream Bridge*, that's what they are calling it, Tkacz and Phipps, co-translators, as previously mentioned. And it's easy to see why, once you drown in the poems: the poems are "bridges" to "dreams." (It's also true that (spoiler alert!) if Lysheha were still alive, he'd be laughing uproariously at someone (in this case, me) writing anything so academic, so pedantic, as an "Introduction" to his poems, in that they themselves resist interpretation to the death, dagger clenched between the teeth.) But I digress.

But perhaps digression is the only means of approach? For example, his unique, dare I say gymnastic, punctuation reinvention? YOU MUST (assuming you are our man, Lysheha) ALWAYS USE TWO (2) PERIODS. Because then you are where you should be, at the party where we did/didn't meet and the (spoiler alert) time we did meet in Kyiv and then he (you) died, all wrapped/rapt up in nakedness.

Because..

Two periods is smack between the sentence and the ellipsis. Two (2) periods instead of one (1) both emphasizes the finality of the Sentence while at the same time approaching the eternal on-goingness of the ellipsis's three (3) dots. Not to mention the use of a period to introduce a question mark or exclamation point as needed, a single period holding the sentence while ? and ! move in to do their work, e.g. .? and .! (Does that sentence need a period at the end?) All this grammatical innovation charges the page with weirdness, doubt, bravado, awkwardness, naïvte, and yes, a bridge to dreams.

Came in with a batch of poems under his overcoat, you could hear them, begging to be read. Wandered in wearing bathing trunks and suggested we all go "fishing for poems." Started quoting Shakespeare in Ukrainian, saying this was the language the work was written in originally, that the notion they were composed first in English is an elaborate hoax!

"goodnight, shakespeare..
we did not recognize you.."
"goodnight.. goodnight.. goodnight..
you did not recognize me?—well, it's me.."

(Remember again the "me" is Oleh..)

"The words I use and the way I walk are pantomimed.."

"For this book.." Only the best of each period of his poems, his life, was to be included, due to production costs and academic assertions. Ghosts and dreams and the cow itself all in. Calmly stepping into the river, drowning. The party-goers transform into animals—hawks, ravens, bears, wolves, deer, swans, and one hundred and thirteen (113) varieties of fish, of which an even baker's dozen (13) being types of herring.

On the other side of the bridge, Paleolithic horses are speaking from cave walls and old illiterate Hutsul women kibbitz Lysheha's poems and guard Franko's spirit.

Transformation

Surely, the whole lot of revelers were not transformed into fish, flapping gills in hilarity while sucking in vodka with their pouty lips?

From then on, on the Lower East Side, far as I can tell, it was only Lysheha's poems that held space. Wandering through, requiring the theatre pay attention, flooding Virlana's dreams. "Mountain" was first, showed up at Yara soon after the company was formed 1990, the search for old blacksmith shops through the Carpathians. The smithy's widow still lives there, she'll tell you about Franko's visits, yes, Franko, the great poet, he started as a blacksmith, you didn't know that? On stage the mountain is always there, and, following the old woman's directions, Franko might lead Lysheha to certain berry patches, a white stone on which this very poem was written, and then children's voices, singing on up ahead.

Another of course was "Swan," and here things get a bit more complicated, in that maybe he was drunk, or maybe he ran into a drunk, and maybe that was him. But in any case, he was playing hide and seek with the moon through the pine trees—I'm only telling you this based on the Yara production, which must have been, when? Maybe 2003. Was the actor Yuri Shevchuk? Andrew Colteaux! Of course! At any rate, the road, the very road that Lysheha walked on, slipped from under him and he was in the water which could have been a puddle (or the rain?) and was also slipping, slipping (the theatrical embellishments that Virlana pulled off at this point being pure magic). The only reference point: a shot glass "someone" had left by the trail. Doesn't matter. Oh, and the bicyclist shadow puppet of course. And its shadow. Next, the whole world disappeared down the road where no one will walk again. Which brings up the shoes, the dang shoes from Danzig, held together by wires, and the ones in the museum known as "slippers" (pointy and beautiful, Lysheha wanted to let us in on the fact that at some point he himself had actually worn them, having found them in a funeral urn, which seems highly suspect, they seemed made for "slipping"). That's how, slightly tipsy, we continue down the road, past the funeral urns of the young girls who had eaten the wild boar meat, past the holes where amber had been found and that the foxes had then deepened, which is where, past where land ends, the Swan will finally appear. Also, Lysheha, the poet, now naked, is pulled into the sea, actually embracing the entire ocean at once (this is all true), and that was that I suppose. Because when Lysheha would walk the road again later, running into himself, an old woman who was all legs, maybe buying some eggs, maybe playing the old hide and seek with the moon, bicyclist, shot glass, maybe up and down the mountain, and of course not even knowing if it was a Swan at all. Makes you stop and think, doesn't it? Ah, Poetry! Ah, Oleh Lysheha. Ah, Maestro!

We left Kolomiya, where John Smith found his shipbuilder, this is true, Google it. We were preparing for/rehearsing/devising *Captain John Smith Goes to Ukraine*, another of Virlana's Yara productions, and such research she did. Of course we knew Kolomiya is better known as the Pysanka Capital of Ukraine. There's even a museum in the shape of an egg, painted like the famed Ukrainian hand-painted Easter eggs. Next, we pulled off the road towards Kamianets-Podilsky. Not for

Captain John, but because this was also a personal pilgrimage for me. Kamianets is where my grandfather, Solomon Geller, was born. (My father, Benjamin Franklin Geller was born in Harlan, Kentucky). I scribbled the words down on a scrap of paper the day he met his great-grandchild Sophie, our first baby. Solomon and his wife Sophie (Rothschild, not those Rothschilds) left Kamianets, immigrating to the US in 1922. Virlana the Ever-Vigilant had set up a meeting with a local historian and the next thing I knew she was pointing out back, behind the coffee shop, at an empty lot. "This was where the Geller (pronounced "gay-lar") house was," she said. "It was the first place bombed in the Second World War." I fainted, fell down, was out for a while. Twenty-three thousand Jews from this town were killed during the Final Solution. We would see the castle down the hill, almost a cartoon in its perfection, and spent the night in the Himalayas (the walls were painted with sparkly mountains), taking turns with the octopus (the Japanese drawing in the bathroom of Tamara). We traveled back to Lviv for that fateful night.

Lviv. Long day rehearsing, dinner at the fabulous varynyky joint, Puzata Khata (Belly Hut). Cold, dank, sleety outdoors. Inside communal apartment, the Lviv version of Virlana's East Village flat, friendly, worn-out, wearing sweaters and blankets—this is Lviv, after all. Rehearsal always spills over into the art of talk into which, unannounced and unexpected, the overcoat! Oleh is here.

What is a poet but a human? With a cigarette, piercing gray eyes (hawk) but warm (rabbit) and welcoming (bear). It was a chess match, with the cast as pieces, trading roles and moves. Yes, arrows were slung and swords of words. "There will be no conquering," Oleh chortled. The wine was drunk and the cigarettes smoked. Kasha kasha kasha. The closet doors swung open and the bear entered, etc. The etc. went on a long time, actually, and, for a closing, he read poems. With Virlana directing, and Julian and Susan providing a score. Mesmerizing and nutritious, unbelievably day to day. A ray split the curtain.

The hawk, diving down towards the road that the wild boars ripped apart during last night's crazed orgy, what else could this signify but the end of summer? Don't take my word for it, I'm just quoting Lysheha. And don't ask him either. Anyway, he just left, muttering, "Go.. Read the poems.. As for me, I can't do much else for you, I'm afraid.. Read the poems.." Now I suggest the same. And if you come back, and I hope you do, perhaps you'll tell me all about it, as I have tried to do here.

Bob Holman

Los Angeles, 2021

ЗИМА В ТИСМЕНИЦІ

from WINTER IN TYSMENYTSIA

ПІСНЯ 212

Так багато суперзірок, порослих очеретом..
Десь там Том Джонс
Співає про зелену-зелену траву..
В таку ніч місячними борами
Водять хороводи опеньки,
Притрушені цинамоном..
Як би я хотів пуститись знову
Тим Чумацьким Шляхом назад,
Поорати ще теплий пил..
В таку ніч
Відкриваються найбільші оперні театри –
Для тих, хто в морі, для тих, хто не спить
Елла Фітцджеральд
Мажеться глиною голубою..
Ми не пропадем у цьому світі!..
Ніколи, ніколи не сумуватиму –
Зовсім як дерево низенько над водою..

SONG 212

There are so many superstars, overgrown with weeds..
Somewhere Tom Jones
Is still singing about that green-green grass..
On such a night under the moon among the trees
Cinnamoned mushrooms
Practice choreography..
And I think I want to set off
Back into the Milky Way,
Churn up that warm dust..
On such a night
The grandest operas play for free
To those at sea, to those awake
Ella Fitzgerald
Smears herself blue singing
We shall not perish of this earth!..
No, no, no don't you cry—
Like a willow weeping over water..

ПІСНЯ 2

Це містечко вночі по мені
Заграє на губній гармоніці..
Мене тут не буде..
Я знаю, коли сплю, перекривлює в гримасах
Мої слова, мою покручену ходу..
По площі кінь тягне будку з хлібом: цок, цок..
Ця застигла лава під ногами
Змушує тверезіше дивитись вперед,
Роздирає повіки..
Я відчуваю, десь під ногами
Вночі щось сталось, може, вчора..
Глибинний, неясний гул..
Щоб почути його,
Щоб розбудити в серці
Голос далекого пробудження,
Мусиш заснути,
Вдати глибоку втому..
Кінь з дощаною будкою
Вперто бореться з часом:
Цок, цок – сьогодні білий хліб, гарячий..
Колись і я змагався з часом..
Він підхоплював мене смерчем,
І крутив як хотів високо над дахами..
Тепер я знаю, він замкнутий, темний,
Тісний, як хліб у будці,
Дощанім серці..

SONG 2

When I leave this little town
Harmonicas will play all night long..
But I won't be here..
I know that as I sleep
The words I use and the way I walk are pantomimed..
In the square a horse drags a wooden cart full of bread: *clack, clack*..
Hardened lava underfoot
Makes me take a good hard look
Forces my eyes open..
And I feel that something's afoot
That something has just happened, maybe yesterday..
All that remains is a deep, far-off rumbling..
But before your heart rouses
To the sound,
You must fall asleep
Give in to a deep fatigue..
The horse with the wooden cart
Stubbornly fights time:
Clack, clack—today's fresh bread, warm..
Once I, too, struggled with time..
But it would only grab me in its whirlwind
And spin me high above the rooftops..
Now I know it's small, contained,
Unseen, like the bread in the cart's
Wooden heart..

ПІСНЯ 4

Ще залишився великий цебер без дна..
Ще коли поритись в шухлядах,
Можна вколотись голкою..
Неперсток без дна..
Ще за моєї пам'яті свіжопофарбовані шкіри
Розпростерті на печі, по підлозі..
Все пахне виправою, хутром і хлібом..
Зимо, не йди від нас..
Ще вчора мені розповідали
Про сильця, капкани довкола Тисмениці–
Там лис, там борсук витягнув скривавлену лапу..
Не йди від нас –
З-під Надвірної принесу на собі тобі гори
І оточу високо..
Приведу тобі вітер з Дністра..
Не йди від нас..
Хай уже всі довкола і сіють і орють,
І цвітуть сади,
А ти будь з нами..
Мисливці вертаються, гавкають пси..
І знов з порожніми руками..

SONG 4

All that's left is a big bucket without a bottom..
When you rummage through drawers
Wearing a thimble that doesn't have a top..
You can pierce your finger tip with a needle..
Even I can remember freshly dyed leather
Spread out on the stove and floor..
Everything smells like tanning, fur and bread..
Winter, do not leave us..
Just yesterday, someone told me
About the snares, the traps around Tysmenytsia—
Over there a fox, and there a badger pulled out its bloodied paw..
Don't leave us—
I'll bring you mountains from beyond Nadvirna,
That will tower around us..
I'll bring you wind from the Dnister River..
Don't leave us..
So what if everyone is plowing and sowing
And the orchards are blooming,
Stay with us
Dogs bark, hunters return
With empty hands..

СНІГОВІ І ВОГНЮ

from TO SNOW AND FIRE

ГОРА

Якось під осінь
Мене з товаришем занесло в гори.
Він шукав там сліди давніх кузнь..
Я ж був радий всякій пригоді..
При дорозі перша кузня, відразу за Косовом –
Її відімкнула жінка..
Тісно – якраз щоб розмахнутись молотом..
Ще чути сажею.. по стінах темний інструмент..
Чоловік недавно вмер.. жінка вийшла..
Вона вже не боялась, що там щось пропаде..
У Криворівні ми перейшли річку.
Нам показали хату під горою –
Там ніби жила стара жінка,
А як нема, то десь недалеко.. треба почекати..
Ми сіли на траві.. жінка щось косила,
Бо підійшла з косою і стала над нами..
Це ж треба було так далеко йти,
Аби просто посидіти на траві..
Для неї ми, неозброєні нічим, серед білого дня
Були хіба їдким димом,
Далеким відголоском кількох воєн,
Що так само відривали її від роботи,
Лише аби трохи передихнути,
Бо за якийсь час розвіється той дим,
І знов треба робити своє..
Вона й не думала запросити нас до себе –
І не тому, що, може, була скупа –
Там нічого і не могло бути, крім ложки пісної кулеші –
За тими чорними задимленими дверима
Ховалась її самітна нора,
Куди, як зайде сонце, впустить лиш її одну на ніч..
Чоловік так само був ковалем..

MOUNTAIN

It was almost autumn
When my friend and I were drawn to the mountains.
He was looking for abandoned blacksmiths' workshops..
And I was up for adventure..
The first smithy was just past Kosiv,[1] right near the road—
A woman opened it for us..
It was tiny—barely enough room to swing a hammer..
You could still smell the soot.. blackened instruments hung on the walls..
Her husband had just died.. the woman left us alone in the workshop..
Now it didn't matter if anything was stolen..
In Kryvorivnia[2] we crossed a stream.
Someone pointed out a house at the foot of the mountain—
An old woman lives there,
If she's not in, she's somewhere nearby.. just wait..
We sat down on the grass.. The woman was out mowing,
She returned with a scythe and stood over us..
Came all this way to sit on the grass..
We showed up in the middle of the day,
Like some irritating smoke,
A distant echo of the wars
That had also pulled her away from work,
But just for a little while.
Smoke disperses,
And you return to your chores..
It never occurred to her to invite us in—
Not because she was stingy—
There were probably only a few spoonfuls of cornmeal mush in the house—
Black, smoked doors
Hid her burrow,

[1] A town near the Carpathian Mountains.
[2] Village in the Carpathians, where a group of Ukrainian writers spent their
     summers at the turn of the 20th century.

А де кузня? – Згоріла у другу вóйну.. там..
Трохи далі, де показувала її рука –
З кропиви виглядав обгорілий фундамент..
Купа заржавілих гаків.. ковані цвяхи..
Циганський міх був на місці –
На залізних ребрах зогнилі рештки вовни –
Видко, був колись обтягнутий шкурою великого звіра..
Але тепер більше подібний на здохлого чорного пса..
– А у вас тут ведмеді є?
Жінка подивилась і нічого не сказала..
Її погляд не заперечив..
Але вона не мала права казати..
– А Франко був у вас?..
Вона знов подивилась, так само..
І опустила очі: – Аякже, був.. звідси пішов
На ожини.. пішов отако – вона зіщулилася
І притисла до грудей праву руку.. –
На тім каменю сів ще спочити..
За кільканадцять кроків поперек стежки
Білів плаский камінь..
Вона знов подивилась на нас –
В її очах була певність: ви його не догоните..
Аби не знати як бігли.. він там не пропаде..
Навіть коли й не вернеться..
Гора добра.. прийме до себе..
Тим більше, такого скаліченого чоловіка..
Звідти верха не було видно,
Лише темна заросла густо ожиною стіна..
Вгорі чути голоси..
Десь аж на небі кричали діти..

And when the sun sets they admit only her for the night..
Her man had been a blacksmith..
"And where's the smithy?" "Burned down in the second war.. Over there."
Where she pointed,
Charred remains stuck out of the nettles..
Some rusted hooks.. hand-forged nails..
The bellows were in place—
The iron ribs were covered with rotten bits—
Once, they were covered with the skin of some large animal..
But now they resembled a dead dog..
"Do you still have bears here?" we asked.
The woman looked at us, but didn't reply..
Her look didn't contradict us..
But we sensed that she felt it wasn't her place to talk about it..
"And Franko,[3] was he ever here?"
She gave us the same look again..
Then lowered her eyes. "Sure, he was..
Went to gather blackberries.. that way," she squinted
Then she clasped her hand to her chest..
"He sat down to rest on that rock.."
A little further up the path
A flat white rock glistened..
She looked at us again—
Her eyes spoke confidently: "You won't catch up to him..
No matter how hard you try.. He won't perish..
Even if he'll never return..
The mountain is kind.. it will embrace him..
Someone so wounded.."
We couldn't see the top of the mountain,
Only a sheer cliff overgrown with blackberries..
Somewhere above we heard voices..
Children shouting into the heavens..

---

[3] Ivan Franko, (1856-1916) one of Ukraine's greatest writers, was the son of
     a village blacksmith.

ВЕДМІДЬ

Повечерявши при місяці,
Кожну кістку склав акуратно –
Меншу до меншої, більшу до більшої
На ще теплій землі –
Ану ж прийде чоловік і йому заманеться
Просвердлити одну
І змайструвати з неї сопілку..
І привітати інший ранок..
А так усе ніби те саме –
Темніє дикий часник, наливається ожина..
Його лапа ще досить страшна,
Щоб захистити цю ніч..

BEAR

After dining in the moonlight,
He sorted the bones—
The small and the larger separated accurately
On ground that was still warm—
What if someone should come along and decide
To carve a hole in one
And make a flute..
To greet the dawn..
Otherwise things were the same—
The wild garlic was growing darker, the blackberries were filling out..
And his paw was still strong enough
To protect the night..

ЯСТРУБ

– А куди веде ця дорога?
– Та перейдете через одне літо,
Далі минете ще одне, менше,
І ще менше – там буде село Погоня..
..Бита польова дорога, розтріскана, як черепок,
Довкола сама червона конюшина і хмари..
Хтось загубив оберемок вівсяної соломи –
Прямо посеред дороги..
Присяду трохи.. ще йти і йти..
Не дає спокою джміль.. тут твоя нора?..
У мене немає нектару..
Чи подаєш мені тривожний знак?..
Та йду вже, йду!..
Відразу за спиною звихрюється смерч
І хапає солому..
Під горою пасеться ціла череда свійських голубів,
І коли злітають проти сонця –
З неба раптово осипається риб'яча луска..
Далі, щоб хоч трохи сховатись у холод,
Пішов навпростець
Кукурудзою, «кінським зубом» –
Боже, як понівечили її вепри!
Надкушені, виплюнуті качани..
Закривавлені згустки шерсті після нічного шабашу..
Куди ж заведе ця порита іклами дорога?.
Невже додому?..
А де ж твій дім.. може, яструб знає? –
Розчепірені крильця прозорі,
І посередині темна цятка, як у метелика,
Що завис на ціле літо над горою..
Але бач? – урвалося літо –
Він похитнувсь.. іди за ним..

HAWK

"Where does this road lead?"
"If you walk for one whole summer,
Then a little less the next,
And then even less the following year—you'll find a village called Pursuit..
..Packed dirt road, with cracks like a piece of pottery,
Surrounded by red clover, and clouds..
Right in the middle of the road—
There's an armful of straw that must have fallen off a wagon..
I'll sit down, there's still a long, long way to go..
But a bee won't let me rest, "is your nest here?..
I don't have any nectar..
Are you warning me?..
Alright, I'm going, I'm going!.."
A whirlwind picks up behind my back
And grabs the straw..
A flock of pigeons feeds at the foot of the mountain,
When they fly up into the sun—
Fish scales suddenly fall from the sky..
A little further, looking for some shade
I walk straight through
A field of Horse-tooth corn—
Lord, how the wild boars have torn it up!
It's littered with gnawed, spit out corncobs and
Bloody bits of fur after their wild night orgy..
Where does a road ripped up by boar tusks lead?..
Home?..
Where is home.. maybe the hawk knows?—
His outspread wings are transparent,
With dark spots in the center, like a butterfly,
He hovered over the mountain all summer..
Do you see him? He's diving down—
Summer's ended.. you must follow him.."

ЗАЄЦЬ

Пізнавши битий шлях
І не менш забите узбіччя –
Ним усе життя переганяли худобу,
Ще коли не було фургонів –
Мої податливі, глибокі вуха
По вінця виповнились металевим бряжчанням..
Хто тепер годен прокричати у них,
Де подівся мій дім на узліссі,
Обтиканий прутиками ліщини і дикої черешні..
Може, я не так бігав?..
Може, занадто багато хотів – стати більшим,
Стрибастішим? – чистий, вічно підтягнутий –
Коли, з чого влилась у мене ця темінь чавуну?
Здається, уся моя легкість
Згромадилась в одну велику непорушність
Затвердлої грудомахи землі,
З одного боку трохи подібної
На розбухлу зайчиху з утомленими повіками
В останню ніч перед покотом,
А з другого боку – на слизьку жабку, зайча
У свою першу ніч, коли воно ось-ось попливає
По грудді у далекий неприхильний світ..
Недорозвинуті вуха.. які вони крики почують
Трохи пізніше, пересягнувши де у два скоки,
А де вплав кілька десятків річок..
Обігнавши сотні собак?..
Я не заєць! я не заєць! –
Ти хоч чуєш мене серед поля, яструбе..
Розпелехана копице червоної конюшини?!.

RABBIT

I recognize the beaten path
And the worn out roadside—
Where the cattle were driven,
Before there were vans—
My pliable, great ears
Were filled to the brim with metal rattling..
Who can shout into them now,
Where is my home on the edge of the forest,
That was fenced off with hazel and wild cherry twigs..
Maybe, I did not run the right way?..
Maybe, I wanted too much—to grow bigger.
Jump higher?—be clean, always fit—
When did this cast iron darkness pour into me and how?
It seems, all my lightness
Thickened into one great immovable mass,
A hard lump of earth,
On the one hand like
A pregnant female rabbit with drooping lids
The night before giving birth,
On the other like a slippery baby rabbit
On its first night when it's about to crawl
Away from the breast into an uncaring world..
It's poor undeveloped ears.. what noise will they hear
A little later, after a jump or two,
Or a couple of dozen river crossings..
Or after outrunning hundreds of dogs?..
Hawk, do you hear me—I am not a rabbit!
I am not a rabbit!—out in the middle of a field..
That's just a messy pile of red clover?!.

КІНЬ

Колись я втечу.
Я ще можу вкусити.
Мені допоможуть гори.
Я був там.
На згадку про той час
Чоловік на горбатій стіні
Обвів червоним
Тіні кількох моїх друзів,
Що поволі, один за одним
Опускались на водопій
До підземної ріки..
В моїй гортані
І досі бовтається
Грудка льоду..
Мене ще не забув ліс.
Може здатись,
Що на випаленій землі
Удвох із чоловіком розорюєм попіл
Насправді тягну за собою
Ще дрімучіший ліс,
Бо хто ж тоді я,
Як не його блудний син?..
Я люблю стояти під вільхою,
Щоб на мене сипались
Її чорні шишки –
У нас подібна доля,
Така ж темна, крихка –
Ще кілька таких тисячоліть,
І її не стане –
А поки лише завдяки дарові
Перевтілення може уподібнюватись
Сосні чи іншій

HORSE

One day I'll run away.
I can still bite.
The mountains will help me.
I was there once.
To remember those days
Man outlined in red the shadows of my friends
On the cave wall,
As one by one,
They slowly approached an underground stream
And drank from it..
To this day I can feel
A lump of ice
In my throat..
The forest has not forgotten me.
Sometimes it might look like
I'm plowing with man
The ashes of the scorched earth
When in fact I'm dragging behind me
A forest that is still asleep,
Because who am I,
If not its long lost son?..
I love to stand under the alder tree,
As its black cones
Fall on me—
We share a similar fate,
Dark and fragile—
A few more millennia
And this tree will disappear—
In the meantime, only thanks to the gift
Of transformation can the alder pretend
To be like a pine, or
A person—

Людській істоті –
Хоч насправді вона
Родичка іхтіозавра..
Втомлений сонцем,
Я теж вмію увійти часом
У забутий стіг осоки,
Прив'ялений у холоді
На мочарах – там я
Довго на самоті
Сумним великим оком
Вглядаюсь у дерево навпроти:
Від самого верха по стовбуру
Звивається чорна лінія –
Тиха темна річка спливає,
Обминаючи його гілля..
Вона продовжилась
Вздовж мого хребта..
Буває, чиясь душа заходить
Надто далеко від дому,
І яскравий мох манить її
І затягує до себе
На дно підземної ріки –
Раптом перед нею виринає
Розсмиканий пахучий стіг –
Знайте – то я чекаю,
Поки на сонце не наповзе хмара,
І вже тоді зрушусь
І тихо піду,
Підказуючи тверду дорогу
Заблуканій душі..
Хоч тому, хто заблукав,
Може здатися навпаки –
Що саме у тому далекому,
Забутому усіма стозі осоки –
Вже вибіленому як папір,

Although actually
It is related to the ichthyosaur[1]..
When I'm exhausted by the sun,
I know how to crawl into
A pile of sedge
Decaying in a cool
Swamp—there
Alone for a long time
My sad eyes stare at
The tree facing me:
A black line winds down
From the very top of the trunk—
A silent, dark stream that flows down
Avoiding branches..
It continues
Across my spine..
Sometimes, someone's spirit wanders
Too far from home,
Tempted by the bright moss,
It's lured to the bottom
Of an underground stream—
Then suddenly,
A messy fragrant stack of hay emerges—
You know—it's me,
I've been waiting for a cloud to cover the sun,
But, I move
To quietly lead
The lost spirit down
The safe path through the swamp..
But to someone who is lost
It can seem otherwise—
They see a faraway

---

[1] A prehistoric marine reptile which had a fish-like body, four paddle-shaped flippers and a head similar to a dolphin's.

Чи вже звугленому –
Раптом ворухнулась
Чиясь ще більше заблукана
Самотня душа?
Але хто вже знає тепер,
Що воно таке –
Самотня душа?..
Мій брат тур – чи він знав? –
Злущилась червона вохра на стіні печери
І його не стало..
А мій брат граб,
Теж ніби гордий –
Чи він знає?
Затаєніший, дикіший,
Він бігає ордою,
Тонке, холоднокровне тіло
Ніби вжалене гадюкою,
Сіпаються жили на ногах
І весь залитий холодним потом –
Кого він боїться?
Що його змушує купчитись по горбах
У важкі, задимлені хмари?
Чи він знає?
Собака – той, може, знає..
Він мучиться як ніхто,
Вічно усміхнений,
З великими замріяними очима..
Але земля перед ним
Так само вже розступилася –
І я здогадуюсь, чия тут вина..
Дійсно, я вдячний чоловікові,
Хто колись на згадку
Обвів наші тіні
Червоною і чорною землею,
Підмішавши туди крові,

Long forgotten pile of sedge—
Bleached paper-white
And hard as rock—
Suddenly stir.
What is that?
Can it be an even more lost
Lonely soul?
But today who knows
What is
A lonely soul?
My brother the bison—did he know?—
The red ocher peeled off the cave walls
And he disappeared..
My brother the blue-beech tree,
So proud—
Does he know?
Secretive and wild,
He's part of a pack,
His thin cold-blooded body
Looks snake bitten,
The veins twitch in the roots
He's covered in cold sweat—
What is he afraid of?
What forces him to band together on hilltops
Forming smoky steel-gray clouds?
Does he know?
Maybe the dog knows..
He suffers like no one else,
Always smiling,
He has such large dreamy eyes..
He could sympathize..
But the ground near him
Is also falling away—
I can guess whose fault it is..
Really, I'm grateful to the man

Щоб хоч трохи скрасити
Перед собою дикий камінь.
Але не лише вдячність тримає
Мене тепер коло стійла —
І зовсім не рана, що не гоїться
З того часу в горах,
Коли, вдоволено відступивши від стіни
З долонями в закривавленій глині —
Він раптом зрозумів,
Що по горбатій стіні печери
Наш невеликий табун гнідої масті,
Легко перескакуючи з виступу на виступ,
Втікає від нього назавжди..
І саме тоді злякався, не витримав
І чимось гострим ударив —
Може, побачивши пораненого,
Інші впадуть на коліна?..
Так воно й сталось..
Роз'ятрена рана ние ночами,
Змушує плекати втечу..
Але як лишу його тут самого?..

Who traced our shadows
With red and black clay,
Probably mixing in some blood
To add a little color
To the harsh stone.
But it's not only gratefulness
That keeps me in this stall—
It's certainly not the wound that won't heal
Since the time in the mountains,
When, with hands smeared with the bloody clay,
Man stepped back from the wall, satisfied
And suddenly realized—
That our small herd of bays
Leaping easily from ledge to ledge
On the curved wall of the cave
Was escaping from him forever..
So, he became frightened, couldn't help himself
And struck out with something sharp—
Maybe, he thought the others would fall to their knees
Seeing that one was wounded?..
And that is what happened..
The inflamed wound burns each night,
Forcing me to plan my escape..
But how can I leave him here alone?..

ЛЕБІДЬ

Боже, я відходжу..
Мене вже не тримає на собі ця дорога.
Я вже не такий п'яний..
Місяцю, не тікай..
Вийду з-за сосни – ховаєшся..
Зайду – світиш..
Зачинаю бігти – стоїш за мною..
Стану – нема..
Лише темні сосни..
Сховаюся за сосну – знов ти сам..
Я є – тебе нема..
Нема..
Нема..
Є..
Нема..
Є.. нема..
Я не вмію так яскраво проминати!..
Зачекай.. мені так хочеться
Постояти під тобою..
Може, ти не бачиш мене?..
Ось нога –
Хіба не зблискує дротик на черевику?..
А в ньому не біліє гола кістка?..
Я хочу закурити і не маю..
Нахиляюся і не бачу..
Тут недавно ніби прогупотіли люди
З нічного поїзда –
Невже ніхто нічого не загубив?..
Я допалю за когось..
Дивись – я нахиляюся раз за разом
І обмацую землю..
Ні.. знов щось крихке..
Чиясь порохнява кістка..

SWAN

God, I'm slipping..
This road can't hold me anymore..
I'm not even that drunk..
Moon, come here..
I come out from under the pines—you're hiding..
I go back under the pines—you shine..
I start running—you're at my back..
I stop—you're gone..
Only dark pines..
I hide behind a pine—and you come out..
I come out—you're not there..
Not there..
Not there..
There..
Not there..
There.. not there..
I can't move that fast!..
Wait.. I want to
Stand in your light..
Maybe you don't see me?..
See, this is my foot—
Look, see the wires holding my shoe together?
Don't they sparkle? My naked ankle's so pale it must glisten..
I need a cigarette, but haven't got one..
I look around—nothing..
The night train just stopped here
Maybe somebody
Dropped a butt?..
I could smoke it..
I'll look—I look and look
And feel around..
Nothing.. here's something..
No, just an old bone..

Чому нікого не пошлеш?..
Чому не дзвонить нічний велосипедист?..
Будь ласка, я відступаюся..
Місячна дорога вільна –
Я почекаю..
Отут якось під сосною
Надибав чарку-стограмівку..
Далі дорога розходилась,
А чарка була посередині..
Я лише підніс її і понюхав..
Може, налита мені?..
Тепла.. гранчаста..
Хотів було взяти, але передумав..
Отут уночі якось вирвав із коренем
Суху сосну й поволік..
І коли підтягав її до Глевахи, закрапало..
Мене спинив тихий спів..
На дорозі стояв хтось і розгойдувався..
Те місце над калюжею найтемніше,
Над нею низько якесь деревце –
Не то здичавіла вишня..
Він співав і дивився на воду в піні..
Я протяг сосну через калюжу,
А другою рукою підтримав торбу –
У ній бовталась пляшка
Ніби червоного вина..
Він не відступивсь і далі співав..
Може, треба було там стати
І затягнути разом?..
Може, він знайшов якраз
Те єдине щасливе дерево?..
Ніхто ж не знає, де воно і яке..
І кому дано його знати..
Я ніколи під ним не стояв..
Навіть щоб хоч перечекати дощ

Why don't you send me some company?..
How about a guy on a bike ringing a bell?..
After you—I'll step aside..
The moonlit road is empty—
I'll wait..
Once I found a shot glass
Under this pine..
Where the road splits,
The glass stood right in the middle..
I picked it up and sniffed it..
Maybe someone had left it for me?..
It was warm.. cut glass..
I was going to take it, but then I changed my mind..
In this very spot one night I pulled out a dried-up pine
Roots and all and dragged it off..
And when I had almost gotten to Hlevakha,[1] it started to drizzle..
I heard someone singing softly, so I stopped..
He stood in the road swaying..
In that spot near the puddle, in the shadows,
Where there's a tree with very low-hanging branches—
Maybe a cherry tree gone wild..
He stood there singing and staring at the bubbles in the water..
I dragged the pine through the puddle,
In my other hand—
I held a bottle
Of cheap red wine..
He didn't step aside, but went on singing..
Maybe I should have stopped
And joined him?..
Maybe he had found
The tree of bliss?..
Nobody knows where it grows or what type of tree it is..
Or who is destined to find it..

[1]   A small town outside of Kyiv with a notorious psychiatric hospital

І підглянути, як між краплями
Пухнуть тихі бульби..
Він підвивав і розхитувався на місці..
Дерево його не хотіло пускати..
Інакше б він упав..
Але тоді перестав би дощ..
Він таки витанцював свій дощ
Під тим деревом..
Я не вмію так..
А може.. то був вовк?..
А тут якось між соснами
Оглядалась і бігла старша жінка..
Повні ноги були ще її –
Але вище був лише розкуйовджений
Оберемок півників..
Вони обіймали її шию,
Мляво звисали на плечі..
Заколисані на грудях,
Присипані жовтою пудрою,
Кліпали сонні повіки..
Вона пливла, повна ясна хмара,
І я за нею, гойдаючись
Так само на її грудях,
Засинаю, пригрітий..
Як вона несе поволі
Щось останнє, найрідніше,
Аби заховати у тінь,
Щоб не зайшов надто гостро
В хлипкі, розтулені легені
Цей світ..
І одночасно мені здалось,
Що вона вийшла і тікає
З мого серця..
Раптово зникаючи з цілим світом
По цій дорозі,

As for me, I never stood under that tree..
Not once, not even to wait for the rain to stop
While watching bubbles swell up
Between the raindrops..
He was humming and swaying..
The tree held him fast..
Otherwise, he would have fallen over..
If he had, the rain would have stopped..
His dancing brought the rain
To that tree..
Me, I don't know how to do that..
On second thought.. maybe it was a wolf?..
Right here between the pines
An old woman ran by, looking over her shoulder..
The full legs were hers—
But further up there was only
A frowzy armful of irises..
They clung to her neck,
And feebly hung down her shoulders..
They had fallen asleep at her breast.
Their sleepy eyes were
Dusted with yellow powder..
She floated by, a full bright cloud,
And I also clung to her,
Swaying at her breast,
Falling asleep, warm..
She carried us carefully
Like something precious, dear,
Hiding us in the shadows,
So that our poor, wheezing lungs
Wouldn't fill up too suddenly
With this world..
At the same time, I felt that
She had rushed out of my heart,
Escaping..

Де вже не пройде ніхто..

Мене не було тут цілу зиму..

Я зумів заховатись..

Трохи далі – отам..

За найвищою сосною,

Під Великою Ведмедицею,

Якраз де вона стрімко падає

Головою вниз..

Цієї зими щось розгорілася Венера

І гнала мене все далі і далі на захід..

В Данцігу я ніяк не міг знайти

Хоч якісь черевики –

Бачиш – мідним дротиком перев'язаний

І діра коло великого пальця..

Я всюди заходив і питав,

У кожні важкі різьблені двері

З кришталевим дзвоном..

Але хіба догодиш цій нозі?..

І нарешті зайшов у твій музей

Над самим каналом..

Трохи загрітися, бо не переставав

Їдкий дощ..

А більше не було нікого..

І там у кутку під шклом

Саме підсихала пара задубілих капців

Після того, як відлежали

Десь у багні чи торфі на тому світі,

А ті ноги, колись у них взуті,

Певне, закам'яніли..

З хвилястими зав'язками..

Від них не можна було відірватись..

Трохи далі стояли

Поховальні урни – темні такі горшки

З намальованими очима і вушками,

Проткнутими, мабуть, кістяною швайкою..

Disappearing with the whole world
Down this road
Where no one will ever pass again..
I wasn't here all winter..
I managed to hide out..
A little further up the road—over there..
Under the tallest pine,
The one under Ursa Major,
Where the Big Bear seems to fall straight down
Head first..
This winter Venus was on fire
And chased me further and further west..
In Danzig I couldn't find
Any shoes—
See—I had to wire these together
And there's a hole near the big toe..
I looked everywhere,
Walked up to every heavy carved door
With a crystal bell, and asked..
But do you think you could ever satisfy this foot?..
Finally I walked into this museum
Right near the canal..
I had to get warm at least,
The rain wouldn't stop..
No one else was there..
And in a corner under glass
I saw a dried-out pair of ancient slippers,
Which must have lain in some swamp or bog
On their way to the next world.
The feet they once held
Have probably turned to dust..
Pointy, graceful, with curved straps
I couldn't pull myself away from them..
A little past them stood
Funeral urns—dark pots

І з них звисали грубі мосянжні сережки..
Вони всі були як одна
Велика родина,
Що розсілася десь на галявині у лісі
Пообідати свіжим кабаном..
І я кожну обходив
І оглядав зачаровано..
Гарні.. дуже гарні..
На кожній разки дрібного,
Видко, колотого – як мишачі ікла –
Непрозорого бурштину..
То були урни з душами
Убитих молодесеньких дівчат,
Що після кабана раптово здулись
І в кожної розв'язався пуп..
Чи хтось тепер повірить,
Що я там колись був?..
Що моїй нозі було так вільно
У тих капцях?..
Тоді, після музею,
Вже не було куди дітись,
І ввечері схолодніло,
Зима є зима, хоч і без снігу,
Лише той їдкий дощ,
Я дочекався, поки стихне,
І аж тоді пішов..
Уже темніло,
Я минув низькі покручені сосни,
І під кожною випорпана шахта,
Де колись залягав пластом бурштин..
Але деякі, може, поглиблені
І лисами.. в одну таку нору
Мало не впав..
І їх якось минув..
Вже було темно,

With painted eyes and ears
Pierced with an awl, maybe a bone..
From which hung heavy brass earrings..
They were like one big family
That had just sat down in a clearing
For a picnic of fresh wild boar..
I walked around each one
Examining it, enchanted..
They were beautiful.. very beautiful..
Each one had a necklace of tiny,
Sharp beads, like mouse teeth—
The color of milky amber..
These were the urns
Of young girls who died
After eating boar
Each stomach bloated till it burst..
Would you believe me if I told you
That I once wore those slippers?..
That once my foot was so happy
In those slippers?..
After the museum,
There was nowhere to go,
The evening had gotten cold,
Winter is winter after all, even without snow,
There was only the rain,
I waited for it to stop,
Then I left..
It was getting dark,
I passed some pines with low hanging branches.
Under each tree there was a hole,
Where they once found amber..
Foxes dug and made the holes even deeper..
I almost fell into one..
But then managed to get past them.
It was dark,

Як підійшов до краю землі..
Не було жодної душі,
Лише мокрий пісок..
Я сів.. і довго дивлюся перед собою..
Так тихо..
І раптом з густого туману
Випливає лебідь..
Повернув голову..
І так само згас.. раптово..
Його високо піднята шия
Була останнім променем..
Чи дозволив мені той охоронець увійти?..
А як він подививсь!..
І вже не було нікого..
І тоді зірвав усе із себе і увійшов..
Припливу не було.. ні.. навпаки..
Усе відходило і тягло за собою..
Під ногами раптом осунулося дно,
І я потонув..
І я вивернув очі з самого дна,
І щосили повіками обійняв
Усе відразу море..
Ми були з ним лише
Безмежно розтягнуті очі,
Без дна і неба..
І тепер, коли вертаюся знов
Цією нічною дорогою,
Я ніби ще не стулив ті повіки..
Хто там за сосною мене чекає?..
Знову п'яний і без нічого?..
О, візьміть мої очі..
Я можу вступитися..
Скажи, як можна вийти звідси?..
Лише зайти у тінь за сосну?..
Так легко?..

When I got to where the land ends..
There wasn't a living soul,
Only wet sand..
I sat down.. and stared out for a long time..
So quiet..
Then suddenly out of the thick mist
A swan swam out..
It turned its head..
And disappeared.. Just as suddenly..
That long neck
Was like the last ray of the sun..
Was he the guardian who let me in?..
What a look he gave me!..
There was no one else..
So I ripped my clothes off and stepped in..
It was not high tide.. no.. on the contrary..
It was ebbing away, pulling me out..
Suddenly I felt the sandy bottom give way
And then I went under..
So I opened my eyes wide
And forced my lids to embrace
The entire sea at once..
It was only me and the swan
Eyes wide open,
Not bound by a bottom or a sky..
Now, when I walk
Down this road again at night,
It's like I'm still there and
My eyes are still wide open..
But who's behind that pine?..
Some poor drunk?..
Please, take these eyes..
I'll step aside..
Tell me, how do I get out of here?..
Just step into the shadows of the pines?..

Але хіба це не назовсім?..
Чи мене давно нема?..
Звідти і не вертавсь?..
А хто тоді вернувсь?..
І в той день.. ні, пізніше,
Я довго не міг зважитися..
Але потім таки відхилив хвіртку
І попросив у Мані яйце..
І в пазусі мав сто рублів..
Вона пішла в курник
І винесла аж три.. а нічого не взяла..
Лише так тяжко подивилась
І каже: однорукий Дергач
Лишив тут недалеко свою хату
І ходить тепер просить у поїздах..
Як сумно..
А в нього завжди були
Такі спокійні ясні очі..
Ця дорога знов і знов кудись веде..
А я вже відходжу..
Куди змучений чоловік вночі
Може відходити після моря?..
Що йому лишилось?..
Хіба що гори..
Як тяжко опускатись і підніматись..
Я мацаю на землі,
І знов лише тіні сосон..
Я переступаю щораз ту саму сосну..
Вже починаються гори?.
Чи то був лебідь?..
Як він підніс шию..
І заслонив навіть небо над морем..
Не знаю.. я лише ввійшов і відходжу..
Дивись, я розкинув руки
І підіймаюсь до тебе..
Боже, я падаю..

Can it be so easy?..
But that will be my final move, won't it?..
Maybe it wasn't me
Who came back from there?..
Well, who came back then?..
On that day.. no, it was later,
It was a long time before I would've dared to..
Yes, it was later when I opened the gate
And asked Manya for an egg..
I had a hundred rubles in my pocket..
She went into the hen house
And brought out three eggs.. and didn't even take a cent..
She said: Derhach, the guy with one arm
Who lived up the road, abandoned his house
Now he begs on the trains..
She gave me a knowing look
What a pity..
He always had such calm, clear eyes..
This road always leads some place again and again..
And I'm leaving..Where can a tired man go at night
After he's been to the sea?..
What's left?..
Maybe the mountains..
But going up and down is so hard..
I touch the ground,
Only shadows of pines..
I always step over the same pine..
Is this the foot of the mountains?..
Was it a swan?..
How he raised his head..
Blocking the sky over the sea..
I don't know.. I only stepped in and now I'm swept away..
Look, I fling out my arms
And I'm rising towards you..
God, I'm falling..

ВОРОН

Коли сіяли цю траву – вчора? сьогодні? –
А бач – вже зійшла..
Цікаво, чи просо моє зійде? –
Я сипнув десь тут його, під вікном..
Як низько похилилась вишня..
За нею – цілий гай молодих ясенів,
Далі високі берести,
А за ними вже стіна..
Піду візьму щось на обід –
Може, якусь рибу чи сире яйце..
Коли виходив із Лаври,
Майстри вже дотиньковували мур..
А вище над ним дах побивали ґонтом,
І він світився на сонці
Навіть ясніше за підновлені бані
Церкви Всіх Святих.. сяйво м'якше..
Так світиться ще хіба ячмінна солома..
Збоку якась дівчина білить..
Сама.. видно, учениця..
Чи за якийсь гріх..
Виблякла майка висить
На худих плечах, у мокрих темних плямах..
Лівою весь час відкидає волосся з очей..
І, здається, плечі здригаються..
А захляпана вапном рука
Ніяк не може дотягнутись до стіни..
Підійди.. може, якось поможеш..
Вже мало.. чи я проти?..
Та я отак би став тут і білив, білив
Аж до самої смерті,
Аби хтось приносив хоч якусь юшку..
Тут би і жив, під цими берестами..
Для них же білиться ця стіна..

RAVEN

When did they sow this grass—yesterday? today?—
Look—it's coming up already..
I wonder if my millet will sprout?—
I scattered the seeds somewhere here, beneath the window..
The cherry tree bends low..
Behind it—a grove of young ash trees,
A little further stand tall elms,
Beyond them the wall..
I should go get something for lunch—
Maybe some fish or eggs..
I walk out of the monastery,
The workers are finishing the work on the wall..
They are covering its roof with shingles,
That shine in the sun
Even brighter than the polished copper domes
Of the Church of All Saints.. a softer sheen..
Like barley straw..
On one side a girl is whitewashing the wall..
Alone.. probably a student..
Or maybe she is doing penance for some sin..
Her faded T-shirt has dark wet stains
And hangs on her narrow shoulders..
She constantly brushes the hair away from her eyes with her left hand..
Her shoulders seem to shudder..
But her paint splattered hand
Never quite reaches the wall..
Walk up to her.. help her..
Not much left to do.. I wouldn't mind..
Just stand there and paint and paint
Till I died,
If only someone would bring me some soup..
I could live here, under these elms..
The wall is being whitewashed for them..

А для кого іще?.. на біленім її тлі
Дерева і глибші, і вищі..
Я перейшов дорогу..
Там товпились люди.. свіжі персики..
Я став за молодою жінкою..
Вона тримала попід руку плетений кошіль,
У нім на дні трохи одягу..
Вітер підвіяв хустку з шиї..
Яка вона бліда..
Чи її торкались чиїсь вуста?..
Ти, видно, довго йшла до Лаври..
Але й тебе спокусили
Свіжі персики.. ти їх не боїшся?..
Вона якось неспокійно повела шиєю
І за нею раптом забіліла стіна..
Ні.. не буду стояти.. вони ще зелені..
Зайшов усередину..
Оселедці якісь іржаві..
Сіль повилазила на ребрах,
М'ясо повідставало від кісток..
Часом хочеться чогось такого..
З самого дна.. Ні, сама ропа..
Назад Лаврським провулком..
Під акаціями там глиняна стежка
Зі слідами дощових червів..
Постояв, дав старому білому голубові
Напитися з калюжі..
Він пив і пив, як корова.. не відриваючись..
Далі зайшов по груди і скупався..
Злетів – і на церкву Спаса,
Аж на самий верх..
Може, зайти?..
За чавунною брамою яблука білий налив..
Ще висять..
І вздовж доріжки, вимощеної цеглою,

Who else?.. With her in the forefront
The trees seem denser, and taller..
Across the road..
People crowd around.. waiting for fresh peaches..
I get in line behind a young woman..
She holds a woven basket under her arm,
With some clothes in it..
The wind lifts the scarf around her neck..
How pale..
Have anyone's lips ever touched her?..
"You probably walked far to get to the monastery..
But even you are tempted
By fresh peaches.. aren't you afraid of them?.."
She moves her neck anxiously,
And suddenly the wall glows white behind her..
"No.. I won't stand in this line.. those peaches are probably still green.."
I'll step inside the store..
The herring looks rusty..
The ribs are crusted with salt,
The meat separated from the bones..
Sometimes you want something..
From the very bottom of the barrel.. Nothing but brine..
Back down the monastery alley..
Under the acacias there is a clay path
With signs of earthworms after the rains..
I stand there, and watch an old white dove
Drink from a puddle..
He drinks and drinks without stopping.. like a cow..
Then he steps into the puddle up to his chest to bathe..
And he flies up—to the very top
Of the Church of Our Savior..
Maybe, I should go inside?..
Behind the cast iron gate..
Juicy pale apples still hang..
Wild irises

Цвітуть блідо-фіолетові й жовті
Дикі півники..
Я там недавно був усередині,
Там рибалки тягнуть з човна сіті,
І їхні лиця, і човен, і все небо
Дрібно поцюкані сокирою,
Так, ніби їх заскочив чорний дощ..
Чорний залізний дощ.. але ще світяться
Їхні великі розгублені очі..
І хмара, ніби інша, більша сіть,
Оплутала їх разом з їхнім небом..
Як страшно.. поцюкані сокирою,
Стікаючи кров'ю, засліплені,
Знов і знов закидають у бурхливі хвилі
Пошматований невід.. і сподіваються..
Нащо я туди заходив..
У майстрів був обід –
Вони, видно, так і не злазили на землю,
А сиділи на дерев'яній ґалереї
І закушували.. ті, що не пили,
Трохи глибше,
Лежали на дошках і гуляли в карти..
Тої дівчини між ними не видно..
Але низ стіни трохи не добілений..
Може, ще прийде.. а може, й ні..
А хто буде закінчувати?..
Хоч би й ти..
У мене своя покута..
Згорбившись від спеки, голодний,
Добрів до Економічного корпусу..
Навпомацки довгим низьким коридором..
Попід стіною залізні сейфи, хоч би не впасти.
З кожним днем Лавра стає
Якимось бункером.. коли йдеш,
То луна як у тюрмі..

Bloom light lavender and yellow
Along the brick path..
I've been in there and saw the image.
Fishermen pull nets into their boat,
Their faces, the boat, and the entire sky
Are covered with fine hatchet marks,
As if they had been caught in a dark rain..
A dark iron rain.. their great wide-open eyes
Seem lost but still shine..
And a cloud, an even greater net,
Has caught both them and their sky..
How horrible.. all cut up by the hatchet,
Streaming with blood, blinded,
They throw the torn sweeping net
Into the stormy sea again and again.. and hope..
Why did I walk in there..
The workers are having lunch—
They don't climb down,
But sit on their wooden scaffolding
Drinking and eating.. those who don't drink,
Lie on the boards
Further in, playing cards..
I don't see the girl..
But the bottom section of the wall isn't finished..
Maybe she will return, or maybe not..
Who will finish it then?..
What about you..
I have my own penance..
Hunched over by the heat, hungry,
I make it to the monastery's office..
I grope my way down the long corridor..
Lined with steel safes so that I wouldn't fall..
Every day the monastery feels
More and more like a bunker.. my steps
Echo like in a prison..

Доповз до своєї келії
І впав на стілець..
Ну що ж, і ми пообідаєм..
Я витяг з торби те, що мав із дому:
Трохи хліба, олію..
Ножем розпанахав консерву
І виставив на стіл:
Яскрава етикетка на золоченій банці –
А в ній у червоному винному соусі
Згорнулася клубком зграйка верхоплавок..
Тепер можна кликати Івана..
Але він уже йде..
Його ходу пізнати здалеку,
Він тяжко припадав на скалічену ногу,
І сейфи двигтіли, як він
Обходив темні ніші..
Останній ключник Лаври..
Ми мовчки сіли, обоє подумали,
Що могли би скрасити
Цей черствий хліб чимось ліпшим..
І коли я мовчки підвів голову,
Облизуючи томат із ложки,
Раптом відчув, як у нього за спиною
Крізь вікно хтось розглядає нас..
Якась темна гора у шибці..
І побачив у профіль дзьоб..
І тоді перервали обід,
Знов натягли чорні халати
І вибігли надвір..
Там сліпуче сонце,
І тисячі голих людей з усього світу,
І наше вікно,
Біла розпечена стіна
І на вузенькому бляшаному підвіконні
Згорбився ворон..

I reach my cell
And plop down on a stool..
Time for us to have lunch..
I pull what I brought from home out of the bag:
A little bread, oil..
Pry open the can with a knife
And put it on the table:
There is a bright label on the golden can—
Inside some sardines
In a red sauce..
It's time to call Ivan..
But he is already on his way..
I recognize his footsteps from far away,
He drags his injured leg,
And the safes shake
As he makes his way through the dark niches..
He is the last key master of the monastery..
We sit in silence, both thinking,
How can we enhance
The stale bread with a little something..
And as I silently raise my head,
To lick the tomato from the spoon,
I suddenly feel that behind him
Someone is watching us through the window..
There is something dark behind the glass..
Then I see the beak..
So we interrupt our lunch,
Put on our dark work robes
And run outside..
Into the blinding sun
In which thousands of people around the world stand naked,
And in our window,
On the hot white wall
On the narrow metal window frame
A raven hunches over..

Грудьми вперся.. аж вгатився у шкло..
Так, ніби вже впало небо..
А може й не міг далі,
Бо здався без мороки,
І я міцно затис тверде і гостре,
Як сокира, стерно, і пересохлий жмут пір'я..
Ну то що, лісовий самітнику –
Хто мав кого тримати – ти чи я?
Хто мав вирвати мою кістку, ще теплу,
Чорним бородатим дзьобом,
Аби сховати її на обід,
А як зайде сонце –
Випхати її з гнізда на землю під дощ і вітер?..
Ми занесли його всередину
І поклали на підлогу –
Він витягся і завмер..
На ньому не було м'яса,
Лише запах старого, зужитого пір'я..
Я нахилився й отворив дзьоб..
Було незручно, я вкляк на коліно
І побачив запалене горло
І трохи слини по краях..
Язик був у якійсь несвіжій піні..
Так невидимий майже слиз
Осідає на землі ранньої весни
Там, де всякнув сніг,
Пористий і зів'ялий...
Пересохле горло..
Його може зволожити лише свіжа кров..
Але під вечір він ожив,
І вночі Іван його випустив..
Як сьогодні пам'ятаю той день..
В Івана на ранок померла дружина..
Десь, може, через тиждень після того
Ми виїхали в Пущу,

Chest pressed against the glass..
Squashed into it as if the sky had fallen..
Or maybe he just can't fly any further,
He surrenders without a fight,
I tightly grasp the hard breast,
Sharp like a blade, he is nothing but a handful of dry feathers..
So what now, you loner of the forest,—
Who should be holding whom?
Would you have pecked at my bones, still warm,
With your bearded beak,
And hid one for a meal,
When the sun went down—
Only later to push it out of the nest in the wind and rain?..
We carry him inside
Place the raven on the floor—
He stretches and freezes..
He has no meat on him,
And smells of old used up feathers..
I kneel down to open his beak..
It is awkward, I have to kneel on one knee
And see his inflamed throat
With a little saliva on the sides..
His tongue is covered with stale froth..
Opaque as the residue
That settles on the ground in early spring
When the snow melts,
Porous and wilted..
A dried out throat..
That can only be healed with fresh blood..
But by evening he has come to life,
And Ivan lets him out that night..
I remember it as if it were yesterday..
Ivan's wife died towards the morning..
And maybe a week after that
We set out for the Wilderness Reserve,

І в сосновому бору він повів стежками,
Де вона любила гуляти..
У ямах було повно малини..
Ми присіли на поваленій сосні..
Встали і пішли далі,
Підпираючись палицями,
Глибше в малину, кожен сам..
Сосни ставали гіллястіші..
Все вищі і вищі трави..
Долетів якийсь пронизливий крик..
І ніби плюскіт..
За малиною якось несподівано
Забілів пісок, а далі озеро,
Темне і настояне..
І я раптом побачив,
Як багато ховається тут людей!..
Мокрі, мінливі тіла
Зблискують, тремтять.. готові
Спорскнути у бездонну воду
За першим тривожним посвистом..
Зірватися знов у тінь,
І там розгубитися поодинці..
Але як розімліла ця шкіра на дарованім сонці..
Спільні кості повитягалися, пражаться
За густими мурами цієї Пущі..
Посередині озера гойдався човен,
Один-єдиний, чорний проти сонця,
І як не вглядався, не видно
У ньому рибалки..
А може, задрімав на дні..
Я оглянувся за Іваном –
Він зник, але далі, попереду,
Між сосон я впізнав ніби його..
Грубий сук своєю тінню
Розрубав його надвоє..

He leads me through the pine forest,
Over the paths she liked to walk..
The ravines are covered with raspberries..
We sit resting on a fallen pine..
Then stand and walk on,
Leaning on our sticks,
We each make our way separately through the raspberry bushes..
The pines seem more dense..
The grass taller and taller..
Then we hear this piercing cry..
And what seems like a splash..
To our surprise, beyond the raspberries
There's white sand and a little further a lake,
Dark and stagnant..
Suddenly I see,
How many people are hiding there!..
Wet, weak bodies
Gleaming, shaking.. ready
To dive into the bottomless depth
At the first sign of danger..
To disappear into the shadows again
Each one alone..
Their skin lax and the bones stretched out,
As they absorb the gift of the sun
Inside this Wilderness..
In the center of the lake rocks a boat,
Alone, black against the bright sun,
No matter how hard I look I can't see
The fisherman in it..
Maybe he's fallen asleep lying on the bottom..
I turn around hoping to see Ivan—
But he's disappeared, then further ahead,
Among the pines I catch a glimpse of him..
The shadow of a thick branch
Cutting him in half..

Він і далі ловив пальцями малину,
Прогортав її, виринаючи,
То знов ховався і плив,
Виборсувався на сонце..
І мені здалось, він якраз намацав
Ту невидиму стежку,
Що десь перервалася поза нею,
Десь недалеко ще..
Вона ще далеко не відійшла..
Але раптом повернувсь..
І безмежно розширеними зіницями попрохав:
Може, йдем назад?..
Тією самою дорогою побрели назад,
І на тій самій поваленій сосні
Знов присіли..
Дивно.. тут нікого не було..
За нами ніхто не йшов..
Ми ніби там і не були..
Хіба ми були? – я спитав його поглядом..
Він підвів очі,
І я зрозумів.
Ні, я не бачив нічого..
Я купався уві сні, і не знаю
Про ту останню схованку,
Так надійно оточену лісом..
Інакше він знов прилетить..
А тоді, як з'явився у вікні,
Ніби й не було страху..
Лише як притис до грудей
Марне, ледве тепле тіло,
Я заплющився від сліпучої глибини
Бездонного неба над собою,
Над ще не висохлим Лаврським муром,
Скропленим вином тих майстрів..
Ні, страху не було..

His fingers reach through the raspberries,
Raking the branches aside, appearing,
And disappearing, floating,
Emerging into the sun..
It seems to me, that he had just found
The invisible path,
That disappeared with his wife
She is not far away..
Not yet..
Then suddenly he turns..
Eyes wide open and says:
"Maybe we should go back?.."
We return the same way,
We rest
On the same fallen pine..
Strange.. no one else has been there..
No one has followed us..
As if we'd been there and not been there..
Had we been there?—my eyes ask..
He raises his eyes,
Then I understand..
No, I had not seen anything..
I was swimming in a dream, and knew nothing
About that final hiding place,
Surrounded so safely by trees..
Otherwise the raven would fly here again..
But when he appeared in the window,
There was no fear..
He pressed his useless, barely warm body,
Against my chest and then
I could shut my eyes against the blinding depth
Of the boundless sky above me,
Over the still wet monastery wall
That the workers had drizzled with wine..
No, there was no fear..

Ні.. була навіть гордість,
Що на моїх грудях відпочиває
Той мудрий безжальний птах,
Що прилетів аж сюди,
Понад лісами Пущі,
Десь аж звідти, де знов на волі
Бродять біблійні звірі,
Ночують під зорями, паруються,
Минають колодязі,
Раптово покинуті людьми..

No.. there was only pride,
On my chest rested
A wise bird without pity,
He had flown all the way here,
Past the trees of the Wilderness,
From somewhere way beyond,
Where Biblical beasts roam free..
Where they sleep under the stars, as they couple,
And avoid wells
That have been suddenly abandoned by humans..

КУНИЦЯ

– Іди шукай свою дочку..
Видко, знову махнула десь до лісу..
Я знаю, ви обоє чекаєте моєї смерті..
– Чого ти плачеш? – вона ж недалеко..
Походить, погуляє та й прийде..
– Бідне моє серце.. чого ти стоїш? –
Принеси мені трохи меду.. може, хоч засну..
Я приніс їй велику ложку меду
І поклав на стілець коло ліжка.
Вона лежала лицем до стіни.
На її скроні темніло мокре волосся.
Я підійшов і нахилився аж до неї:
– Може, тобі вже перехотілось меду?..
Вона всміхнулась до когось уві сні.
Я вийшов і прихилив за собою двері –
Мене послано до лісу шукати дочку,
Уже вечір, пізно, можна заблудитись..
Але трохи відійшовши,
Я забув про все на світі.
Вона знає, що робить –
У десять років її голова у сто..
Ні, в тисячу раз мудріша за наші!..
Прямо над дорогою заходило сонце.
Так низько, що можна було вже не боятись
І входити в нього..
Кажуть, призахідне сонце лікує серце..
Велике втомлене серце ніколи не забуває
За наші дрібні, сплакані душі..
Лише треба дати знак:
– Ось тут я.. іду вже..
Але коли підійшов до лісу,
То він заслонив навіть сонце.

MARTEN

"Go find your daughter..
She's obviously run off into the forest again..
I know the two of you are just waiting for me to die.."
"Why are you crying? She's somewhere nearby..
She's gone for a walk, when she's ready, she'll come back.."
"Oh, my heart, don't just stand there.
Bring me some honey.. maybe it'll help me fall asleep.."
I brought her a big spoon of honey
And placed it on a stool near the bed.
She lay facing the wall.
Dark hair covering her temples.
I went up and leaned over her:
"Don't you want the honey?.."
She was smiling at someone in her dream.
I closed the door and left—
I was sent to look for my daughter in the forest,
It was getting dark, easy to lose your way..
But after a bit,
I forgot about everything.
She knows what she's doing—
She's only ten years old, but she's a hundred times..
No, a thousand times wiser than we are!..
The sun was setting just over the road.
So low, you could step right into it
Without fear..
They say a setting sun cures the heart..
It's a great tired heart that never forgets
Our small weeping souls..
Give us a sign:
"I'm here.. I'm coming.."
All roads seem to lead to the forest..
But when I approached,
It hid the sun.

Усі ж ніби дороги ведуть до нього..
Хіба я не маю права.. кожен мій крок
Вже лічений.. лише зайду в тінь
І вийду.. ненадовго.. мене ж там, позаду,
Звідки я прийшов, давно вже чекають..
І вже простягнув перед себе руку,
Щоб увійти поступово і чути,
Як тінь втягує до себе голу худу руку..
І в цю мить трохи далі звідти
Вийшов чоловік.. він не був босий,
Але так вийшов тихо, як сновида,
Хоч очі мав розплющені..
Я стояв за деревом і дивився йому вслід.
Він був чорний, невисокий,
Обкиданий якимись іржавими плямами..
Ліс, видно, довго і покірно йшов за ним,
Довго прощався і нарешті став..
Я намацав у кишені ніж
І аж тепер вступив усередину,
В глибоку тінь.. ніби й не бачились..
Але хто знає..
Так виходять з дому ненадовго,
Скоро він буде вертатись,
І треба плутати за собою слід,
Інакше хтось з нас не вернеться..
У темряві під ногами повилась
Висотана, тонша за осоку бліда трава,
І між нею чорна, аж синя, земля..
Впоперек стежки надкушений,
Зі слиною на грубім стеблі молодий часник..
П'ять довгих пір'їн перечавлено
Набряклим важким слідом..
Що має значити ця надкушена
І виплюнута рука.. що далі тобі зась?..
Я підняв очі — за кілька кроків

Don't I have the right.. I'll make each step
Count.. I'll only step into the shadows
And come right out.. I won't be long..
I'm expected back, where I came from..
As I slowly entered
I reached out and felt
The shadows suck in my thin naked arm..
Then just a little further on
A man suddenly appeared, not barefoot,
But he passed by quietly, as if sleep-walking
Except his eyes were wide open..
I watched him from behind a tree,
He was dark, not very tall,
Covered with rust-colored stains..
The forest obediently drifted with him for a while
Then stopped..
I reached for the knife in my pocket
And stepped into the depths of the shadows..
It didn't look like we saw each other
But who knows.. He'd stepped out
The way people step out of their homes for a minute,
And he will return,
So, I should cover my tracks,
Otherwise one of us may never return..
Tall pale grass, finer than sedge,
Spread underfoot in the dark.
The dirt was black, almost blue..
Across the path lay a stalk of young garlic
Bitten and covered with saliva..
The five long blades had been crushed
By a heavy swollen foot..
What does this mean..
Trouble ahead?..
I raised my eyes—a few steps
Off the path loomed a pile

Убік від стежки бовваніла купа
Свіжого соснового гілля –
Може, цей запах завів аж сюди,
В глуху гущавину.. під гіллям стовбур..
Мацнувши його, пальці провалились
В трухлявину, ага – ці гілки тут чужі,
Ними зовсім недавно привалили
Давно вже згнилу сосну.. а може, вона
Серед ночі, в повній темряві світиться..
Освітлює під свіжими соковитими лапами
Теплий, улежаний барліг.. мені здалось,
Вона раптом піднялась і зітхнула,
І ще раз глибоко зітхнула,
Повалилась і знов зітхнула розбурхана
Жива купа глиці, накидана похапцем, навхрест..
Я зайшов у тінь і чекав..
Чекав довго, але ніхто не вертався..
Чи цим дано мовчазний дозвіл
На тимчасовий сховок іншій,
Ще неприкаянішій людині?..
Аж поки хтось не замінить мене тут,
Не перейме ще теплий дух цього тіла..
Але тоді.. куди я тоді подінусь?..
І хто мені вже звідти хоч кивне?..
У високім яснім небі горіли верхів'я,
Несколихнуті, і так само чекали,
Уповивши нагірню дорогу
Найніжнішими пагонами,
Найчистішим світлом..
І там вгорі я раптом побачив,
Як повертається додому куниця
З великою темною жертвою в зубах,
Як вона волочить щось більше за неї,
Що бовталось як намокла торба,
Билось об її груди..

Of fresh pine branches—
Maybe their scent led me into this dense forest..
Under the branches there was a tree trunk
As I touched it, my fingers sank into
The rotten wood, so the branches were not from this trunk,
The tree trunk, long rotten,
Was recently covered.. maybe this pine
Glows in the dark of the night..
Lighting the way for fresh young paws
To a warm comfortable cave.. I felt
The pine tree suddenly rise up and sigh..
Then sigh again, collapsing..
After sighing a third time, it turned into a messy
Pile of fresh branches.. tossed every which way..
I stepped into the shadows and waited..
I waited for a long time, but he did not return..
Was this a silent permission
For temporary shelter for
This restless person?..
Someday, someone else will take my place,
Catching the warm breath of this body..
But then.. where will I go?..
And who would give me a nod from over there?..
The treetops blazed across the endless sky,
Also waiting, they were still,
Creating a canopy that swaddled the road
With their most tender branches
In the purest light..
Then I suddenly saw,
A marten returning home
With something dark she had killed in her teeth.
How did this small furry animal manage to carry
Something so much larger, that swayed like a wet bag,
Beating against her chest..
She was in a rush and did not descend,

Вона поспішала і вже не опускалась на землю,
І вона, і її здобич, вигнувшись,
Перелітали з гілки на гілку,
Щораз глибше і вище провалюючись
У хвилях пругкого листя,
Потемнілого і скропленого росою,
Вона і її жертва, що обвислим,
Просоченим кров'ю клунком
Затулила їй світ..
Я був далеко внизу.
Вона загрібала своїми відчайдушними стрибками
Мене разом з цією зеленню,
З цією тишею глибоко в землю..
Вона заміряла свій кожен кидок
Так переконано і так бурхливо,
Що інакшого виходу вже не було
І не могло бути: вона наздоганяла сонце
І стрибала саме туди, куди підказувала
Їй пам'ять її жертви,
Жертви для сонця..
Хто з нею був? – якась велика птаха,
Що знала точно шлях аж туди,
Але вже не могла летіти?..
І за кого така жертва сонцю –
За всіх нас?.. за мій змарнований
Відтинок часу в потемках?..
Видно, я зайшов уже задалеко
І зовсім збивався з дороги..
Чи мені ще зарано повертатись?..
І ніби вже десь недалеко
Запахло людським житлом і димом..
Я пішов на той запах,
Але то був чужий дим – я заблудився..
Я побачив задвірки якогось лісового села..
Його порожню вулицю, прорубану в лісі..

She and her prey, swooped
Flying from branch to branch,
Landing ever higher, ever deeper
Into the waves of supple leaves
Dark and wet with dew.
She and her prey,
A blood-soaked bundle
That blocked the sight of the world from her..
I was far below.
Her desperate leaps enticed
Me and the foliage
Into a silence deep as the earth..
She calculated every leap
With confidence, impetuously,
There was no other way,
No other choice existed: she was chasing the sun
Leaping where
Her prey's memory suggested,
This was her offering to the sun..
What was it?—some large bird,
That knew the way
But could no longer fly?..
Why was it sacrificed to the sun—
For us ?.. for the time I had wasted
In the shadows?..
It seemed, I had wandered too far
And had lost my way..
Was it too early to return?..
Then I smelled smoke..
There were people here..
I followed the smoke,
But the scent was unfamiliar—I was lost..
I saw the backyards of a forest village..
An empty street cut through the forest..
You could hear a radio playing somewhere,

Десь в глибині озивалося радіо,
Каркала ворона.. низько слався дим.
Я побачив стіни без вікон
І дахи, побиті залізом,
Залізні огорожі довкола..
Але ближче не наважився підійти.
Це було зовсім інше життя..
Далеко за деревами коло останньої хати
Прямо в лісі гойдалась
Напівжінка, напівдитина,
Здалеку важко було пізнати,
Ясно-червона пляма довгої,
Аж до землі, спідниці підлітала
На мотузяній гойдалці, перекручувалась,
І за нею бігала зовсім мала дитина
І пробувала, сміючись, її зупинити..
Потім дитина десь пропала,
І в лісі між дерев зовсім стемніло,
А жінка поволі сама
Гойдалась і гойдалась..
Я повернув назад,
Далі кинувся бігти
І біг, біг, падав,
Підіймався і знову біг..
І коли вибіг, вхопився за останнє дерево..
І тоді я побачив, як підходить назустріч
Поволі, як сновида, той, з ким тоді,
При самому вході розминувся..
Він шукав ніби когось,
Широко розпростерши руки,
Заточуючись, як захмелілий,
Чи приголомшений страшним ударом,
Однією рукою ніби відгрібаючи від себе землю,
А другу заніс над собою,
І в ній я відчув ніж..

A crow cawed.. the smoke lay low,
I saw walls, but no windows,
Metal roofs..
Metal fences..
I didn't dare come closer.
This was a different kind of life..
Near the last house
On the edge of the forest
A woman or maybe a child swung on a swing,
It was hard to tell from far away,
The bright red of her
Full skirt flew up
On the great swing.
A little child ran around
Laughing and trying to grab her..
Then the child disappeared,
It grew dark in the forest
The woman continued to slowly swing
All by herself..
I turned back,
Started to run,
I ran and ran, and fell.
Then got up and ran again..
As I ran out of the forest I grabbed the last tree..
I saw the same man..
I had passed when I entered..
He came towards me..
Slowly like a sleepwalker..
He seemed to be looking for someone,
Flinging his arms..
Staggering like a drunk
Or someone stunned by a great blow,
One hand pushed away the earth,
The other high above
Suddenly I felt the knife..

ДУБ

Кожна галузка затоптана,
Виходжена вздовж і впоперек,
І як вони лише витримують шурхіт воронячих лап?..
Так, наче не привільний сховок, де в прохолоді
Дрімає пташка – а якесь бите роздоріжжя,
Де вічно курява, штурхани, гамір..
Безконечні вечері при заході сонця –
Сиплються додолу кістки,
Недопиті яйця, трохи схожі на гадючі,
Блякле пір' я, рештки смарагдових жуків,
Покраяних вигостреними, аж синіми дзьобами..
Та чи варто дивуватись такій гарячці? –
Просто під дубом дорога,
Нею віддавна снують на фабрику кушнірі,
Досвіта зіщулені в тумані
(Річка спить при самій дорозі) –
Гупають чоботи, брязкають дзвоники
На жіночих роверах – і коли проминають,
В ніздрі б'є гострий дух кролячої шерсті..
Трохи зійде сонце –
І вже річка стає до роботи:
Вода загачена тінями як колодами –
Треба їх розчімхати, вибілити на сонці,
А ще ж треба бігти скоріше на фабрику –
Там вимокають шкіри..
Бідна бджола.. –
Так поспішала на свою зміну,
Що від недосипання (а може, з голоду) –
Запаморочилась голова, і впала у воду,
Але навіть на бистрині,
Як над розквітлою абрикосою –
Дрібно-дрібно тріпоче крильцями, збриживши

OAK

Every branch is worn out,
Damaged by the crows.
How do the branches survive such harsh treatment?..
This is not a cozy place, where a bird can dream
In the breeze—but a busy crossing,
With never-ending dust, noise, jostling..
At sunset comes the devouring
Of bones and half-eaten snake eggs,
That rain down below
Faded feathers, leftover bits of emerald beetles,
Cut with beaks that've been sharpened till they're blue..
This ruckus is no surprise.
The oak stands near a road,
Long used by the furriers heading for the factory
At dawn shrouded in fog.
(The stream sleeps by that very road)
Boots stomp, bells ring
On women's bicycles as they pass
The sharp smell of rabbit fur assaults the nostrils
As soon as the sun rises a little more—
The stream is put to work:
The water is jammed with long shadows
That need to be untangled and bleached in the sun
Run, hurry to the factory—
The pelts are being soaked..
A poor bee..—
In a hurry for its own shift at work and
Dizzy from hunger (or lack of sleep)
Lost its way and fell into the water
But even in the stream
It beats its tiny wings,
As if hovering over a blossoming apricot—

Нервовою павутинкою течію..
..Нема спокою до самого обіду
Аж поки сонце не стане сам на сам
Над цим трохи сумним деревом,
Що тепер мусить рятувати не тільки свої жолуді,
А й прихистити безборонну річку,
І захрипле лоша на дорозі,
По якій недавно прочвалала його матір,
Тягнучи за собою порожній віз —
Усіх має прихистити
Зібрана нарешті у тугий сніп, перев'язана
Жилавими променями, настояна тінь
Віддаленого рідного лісу..
Аж під вечір відпускає їх від себе —
Побіжить відсвіжіла, ніби повноводніша річка,
Підніметься з дна темний короп,
Лоша дожене свою матір,
Промайнуть яскраво на роверах жінки,
Повечеряє, ласуючи яйцями, вороння,
Зайде сонце..
Все ближча, ближча дорога до рідного лісу..
В темному, пухкому небі
Леміші з грубого цупкого листя
Вилискуючи металево,
Прогрібають глибокі борозни,
Привалюючи скибами небо
Із заснулими на льоту птахами —
Падають у ту дрімучу ріллю стрімголов,
Розчепіривши жадібно крила,
В нічний збурений хаос.. —
Додому!..

Fluttering the nervous web of the current.
..There's no rest till lunch
When the sun stands directly
Over this sad tree,
Which now has to protect its acorns,
As well as the defenseless stream
And the snorting foal trotting on the road
Trying to follow his mother who plodded by
Pulling an empty cart—
The oak has to protect them all,
It gathers into a tight sheaf
A shadow infused with the familial forest now far away
And ties it with sinewy rays.
It releases them only in the evening—
That's when the stream runs fresher, and seems fuller,
Dark carp rise from the bottom,
The foal catches up with its mother,
Women on bikes speed by brightly
Crow chicks dine on the tasty eggs
The sun sets..
The road to the familial forest seems closer now..
The dark fluffy sky
Is plowed by dense thick leaves
Sparking like metal, cutting deep furrows,
The sky is covered with
Birds asleep in flight
Passionately stretching their wings
Falling into the dreamscape head first,
Into the shattering chaos of night..
Time to go home!

РІКА

Часом так хочеться побути самому..
І я малим вигріб собі печерку
У березі над рікою,
І в ній, пригадую, сиджу
Навпочіпки і дивлюся на воду..
Повільна Ворона..
Пливе згустками шума,
Здута, як щось утоплене
Чи розквашені, перестоялі гриби..
Бродять, розростаються пухирцями..
Виринають нові..
Поволі, важчі і важчі –
Спливають до Великого мосту..
А навпроти, на тому березі –
Темніє черемха,
І з неї над воду звисає грубий шнур,
Доточений вгорі сталевим тросом..
Під ним глибока яма..
Я сидів там, коли не було сонця, не було нікого,
І перед очима лише той шнур..
Густо пов'язані ґудзи на кінці..
Ніколи, жодного разу
Так і не летів сторч головою..
Підійти і розгойдатись..
І лише розціпити пальці..
Аж тут стиха, ніби раптом –
Спадає дощ.. так, якби чекав..
Чекав, поки не натерплюсь..
І зір не налляється сльозою..
І аж тоді не чути нічого..
Лише як тухне шума
І витанцьовують краплі
На притихлій Вороні..

RIVER

Sometime you want to be alone..
When I was little I dug a small cave for myself
By the river bank,
And I remember sitting in it
Curled up staring at the water..
Of the slow moving Crow River..
Islands of foam floating by,
Swollen, like something drowned,
Or like pickled mushrooms that have been around too long..
Fermenting, blistering..
New ones float by..
Slowly, heavier and heavier—
And drift down to the Great Bridge..
On the opposite bank—
A Mayday tree darkens,
A thick rope attached to a steel cable above,
Hangs from it over the water..
Below there's a deep hole..
I would sit in my cave, when there was no sun, when there was no one,
I'd see only the rope..
Thick knots on the end..
But I never swung on it
Never flew head first..
I should just walk up now, swing back and forth..
Then let go of the rope..
But suddenly the rain starts to fall—
Quietly, as if it had been waiting..
Waiting for this moment
And my eyes fill with tears..
And then silence..
Except for the bubbles of foam dying
And the droplets dancing
On the silent Crow River..

..Що найбільш зворушливе у повінь,
Так це риб'ячий мальок –
Гойдаються хмари намулу,
Перекидаються дерева..
А ці, щойно вилуплені,
При самому березі зійдуться
Де прозоріше, тихше – і дрібними стібками
Одне попри одне вчаться дихати,
Ворушити пірцями..
Стемніли хатки кушнірів
Від безконечного дощу..
Уже давно повні під ринвами
І цебри, і коновки, і кадуби
Для заквашування шкір..
Втомилися і кури, і пес..
Гниє бульба..
Зате вигуділа кукурудза,
Її грубе стебло не боїться нічого –
Ночами давно вже чекає на грім,
Млосно вихиляючи набубнявілим тілом
По коліна у воді..
Пропала конюшина! –
Та, що її шевці, махнувши рукою,
Виміняли за невигідне жито –
Бо таки легше зробити за кілька день
Пару добрих чобіт –
А надвечір вийти під парасолею,
Урвати трохи кролям..
Чи просто постояти –
Подихати, як вона пахне..
Господарство – корова, гноївка..
Ні, все це не для їхніх подовбаних шилом,
Безкровних рук..
А кушнірі –
Хіба є в них коли бавитись з городиною?

..During a flood what is most moving
Are the young fish—
As clouds of silt swirl,
And trees are knocked down..
These just hatched fish
Gather near the banks
Where the water is clearer, quieter—they take tiny leaps
One over the other as they learn to breathe,
To move their fins.
The houses of the furriers have darkened in the endless rain..
The gutters, buckets, watering cans
And tanning vats
Have been full for a long time..
The chickens and dog are exhausted by the rain..
The potatoes rot..
But corn flourishes,
Its thick stalks are fearless—
Waiting for the thunder and lightning all through the night,
Languidly bending its swollen body
Knee deep in water..
The clover's perished!—
The sowers chose her,
Instead of the hard to grow rye—
They think it's easier to make a good pair of boots
In a couple of days—
And then at dusk set out with a parasol,
And pick some clover for the rabbits..
Or simply stand there—
And smell its fragrance..
A farm—a cow, manure..—no,
It's not for them, not for their pale hands,
Used to working with an awl..
Furriers don't have time to play with gardening.
Some potatoes for lunch, maybe some cucumbers..
Things that grow by themselves—

Трохи бульби на обід, якийсь огірок..
Треба, щоб усе само росло —
Яблуко, сливка..
Знайшов піддеревом, витер, надкусив —
Ще зелене, чи трохи підгниле, чи просто не таке —
Розмахнувся і викинув —
Далеко, аж на середину ріки..
Чи ще дальше, аж на той бік,
Аби не полошити рибу..
Смакує — набираєш повні кишені,
Ідеш, випльовуєш сливові кістки у воду..
Кожен має своє черпало навпроти дому —
Кладочку на вербових кілках,
А зійти можна по сходах,
Викопаних рискалем у березі..
В неділю трохи посидіти з вудкою,
Згадати вмерлих..
Але що Вороні до цього?
Чи їй пам'ятати, скільки до Залізного мосту
Вона омила старих жінок —
Які, коли б не корова,
То може так і не забрели у воду?..
Чи того посоловілого пса
З виваленим язиком,
Що кинувся з берега стрімголов,
Як у відчинений навстіж курник —
Аж у воді раптом задумується про свою долю..
І виповзає, здрібнілий, згорблений..
Павучими лапками мацає землю
І йде перед себе, не оглядаючись,
Чимраз далі по розтрісканому глеї,
Гнаний вітром навскіс по стежці —
Ближче до людей,
До мурованих кам'яниць,
Де вже не хапає за хвіст гицель,

Apples, plums..
You find one under a tree, wipe it and take a bite—
If it's too green, or a bit rotten, or simply not right—
Wind up and toss it—
Far into the middle of the river..
Or even further onto the other side,
So as not to frighten the fish..
If it tastes good—stuff your pockets,
You can walk, spitting out plum pits into the water..
Everyone has a water bucket in front of the house—
A plank for a footbridge, tied to a peg
You can walk down the steps,
Carved out of the banks..
On Sundays you can sit with a fishing pole,
Remembering the dead..
What's it to Crow River?
Does it remember how far it is to the Iron Bridge?
The river washed the old women—
Who waded into the water
Because of the cows..
And also that glassy-eyed dog with his tongue hanging out,
Who rushed headlong off the bank,
As if into an open chicken coop,
To realize his fate once he hit the water..
He crawled out bent and crushed..
Touching the ground with his spidery legs
Not looking back, trotting ahead,
Ever further over the silt that's
Chased by the wind diagonally down the path—
Closer to people,
To brick buildings,
Where the dog-catcher won't grab him by the tail,
Where the market still smells of homemade butter
And piglets brought from near Tlumach
Twenty years ago..

А на торзі ще пахне домашнім маслом
І поросятами, привезеними з-під Тлумача
Двадцять літ тому..
Вже давно перестала гупати
Посеред Ринку різникова сокира,
Розрубуючи час
На щораз дрібніші шматки..
Але камінь ще тхне сечею ярмаркового ведмедя,
Приведеного циганами десь аж з-над Дунаю..
Смердить дотепер – а скільки літ минуло,
Як його відвели далі, на Станіслав,
Прихопивши заразом увесь сап'ян,
Дьоготь.. усі кожухи..
Гори каракулевих смушків,
Мішки вовни, чоботи, дубову кору..
Все тихше і тихше риплять їхні мажі..
Заплющившись, Ворона
Минає Великий міст..
Птаха-ріка, що бачила все..
Її тіло пошмагане лозою,
Вимочене у їдкій нафтовій ропі..
Поміж каміння розвіваються
Пошматовані хутра кролів,
Фарбованих під леопарда..
Але що Вороні до того?
Чи хто пам'ятав би, скажімо,
День народження підусти,
Оглушеної кілком на броді,
Як ішла на терло?..
Хіба міг би хто-небудь це пам'ятати?..
Все, все мусиш забути,
Минаючи Великий міст..

It's been a long time since
The butcher's axe could be heard at the bazaar,
Cleaving time
Into ever smaller pieces..
But the stone still reeks of piss from the dancing bear
Brought to the market by the Gypsies from beyond the Danube..
It reeks to this day—though so many years have passed,
Since they took him down to Stanislaviv,
Together with all the kidskin,
Axel grease.. sheep skin coats,
A mountain of Persian lamb collars
Bags of wool, boots, oak bark…
Their wheels grew ever more silent..
Crow River narrows its eyes
As it passes the Great Bridge..
This great bird of a river, sees everything..
Its body full of vines,
Soaked in caustic crude oil..
Ragged bits of rabbit fur,
Dyed to look like leopard
Flutter between the stones..
But what's it to Crow River?
Who would remember, let's say,
The birthday of a fish
Stunned by a stick in the river's ford
As it was heading to its spawning grounds?
Can anyone remember that?..
You must forget it all, you must forget everything,
As you pass the Great Bridge..

ЧЕРЕПАХА

Нюхом я чув – десь тут має бути гриб..
Дуб, мох, волого – десь тут..
Я відійшов кілька кроків убік і рвучко обернувся –
Маневр, щоб не встиг заховатись у траві..
За кущем хтось принишк..
Я опустив голову, знов пішов ніби далі,
Але все ближче, ближче.. ні, то не дубовий лист..
Не камінь.. якась бронзова посудина?..
На високо збитій моховій подушці,
Якраз де впало сонце, розкинувши лапи,
Лежала черепаха..
Може, чиясь.. ніде нікого.. справді, дика..
Якось ще малим раз бачив у Запоріжжі,
В гнилій затоці.. а ця тут, у витоптаному лісі..
Я взяв на руки –
Спідній панцир такий прохолодний..
Кістяна пластина, але жива..
Я би тримав таку ношу вічно,
Аби ти тільки казала, куди тебе нести..
Кістка бліднувата, вичовгана, як долоня, –
Мабуть же там вирізьблені лінія любові,
І дорога, і смерть.. я опустив її знов на мох
І, не оглянувшись, пішов.
..Кілька днів по тролейбусах, в метро
На правій долоні відчував її прохолоду –
А робота для рук завжди знайдеться –
Пиляти, стругати, місити глину..
Мене знов потягло до лісу,
Але проблукавши день,
Так і не знайшов тої місцини..
При дорозі в сутінках маячів мурашник.
Я присів навпочіпки і низько нахилив над ним лице..

TURTLE

I could smell it—there were mushrooms here..
The oak, the moss, the moisture—somewhere here..
I took a few steps to the side then suddenly turned around—
This maneuver was meant to catch something before it managed
    to hide in the grass..
Something took cover in the bushes..
I lowered my head, and feigned walking away,
But actually approached closer and closer.. that was not an oak leaf..
Not a stone.. perhaps a bronze bowl?..
Right in a ray of sun lay a turtle,
With its feet spread out..
Maybe it belonged to someone.. but there was no one.. maybe it was wild..
When I was little, I saw one in Zaporizhia,
In a smelly inlet..
But this one is here, in a forest where many people walk
I picked it up—
The lower shell was so cool..
It's made of bone, but feels alive..
I could carry it forever,
If only you'd tell me, where to go..
The shell was pale, worn-out like the palm of a hand—
Maybe it also has a love line
As well as lines marking journeys and death?
I put it down on the moss
And walked away without looking back.
..For the next few days in trolleys, on subways,
My right hand still felt how cool it had been—
But I can always find work for these hands—
Sawing, carving, or kneading clay..
Later I was drawn to the forest again,
I wandered around the entire day
But could not find the place..

Бистрі, методичні мурашки, здавалось,
Тягали в нору під землею гострі цвяхи..
І раптом моя права долоня
Ніби зовсім окремо від руки впала між них..
Я не міг її підняти, чужу, і вона там заклякла,
Обліплена залізними кристалами,
Покірна, груба, неповоротка,
Далеко від мого обличчя із заплющеними очима..
А бачите, таки не просто прокусити
Мою волячу шкуру..
Як з глибокого колодязя, потрохи запульсувала
Жилами комашина отрута..
Кусайте, кусайте, я стерплю..
..Ранком, прокинувшись, одразу обдивився долоню –
Бліда, мляво натягнута шкіра,
З'їдена милом і роботою..
А може то приснилось, що вона тримала на собі,
Як на моховій подушці,
Покраплену листям і сонцем істоту..
Але нащо тоді вчора
Кинув її в ту озлоблену нору
Поміж мурашок?..

At dusk an anthill loomed near the road.
I squatted, leaning my face low over it..
The methodical ants quickly carried
Iron nails into the underground hole..
Suddenly my right hand
Fell among them, as if detached from my arm,..
I could not lift it, it felt disconnected, it froze up,
Coated with iron crystals,
Submissive, heavy, clumsy,
It felt far away from my face and my closed eyes..
You see, it's not so easy to bite
My thick skin..
The venom of the ants pulsed up my veins
As if from a deep well..
Go ahead bite, bite, I can take it..
..In the morning, when I awoke,
I immediately looked at my hand—
The pale, loose skin,
Worn out by soap and work..
Maybe it was a dream, that my hand held,
Like on a pillow of moss,
A creature covered with leaves in the sun..
But why then
Did I shove it
Into that hole full of
Angry ants?..

ЖАР

Мене таки спокусив ярмарок.
Там буде весело, багато людей —
Колись-таки треба щось продати —
У мене є кілька невипалених глечиків —
От завтра встану раніше, випалю,
А по обіді продам..
Ранком пішов мокрий густий сніг,
Але відступатись вже було пізно..
Я почав стягувати на дно яру повалені дерева.
Граб, навіть спорохнявілий,
Всередині буде твердий, як кістка,
Він сичав, димів, але вогонь є вогонь..
Обсмалений, чорний, я нарешті відкинув пилку
І розігнувся над розпеченою норою
(Це могло бути покинуте лисяче кубло):
Бухкає полум'я, біліє жар..
Орієнтуватись в часі можна лише за сонцем,
Але сніг не переставав,
На дні яру він і довгі мокрі стовбури
Відрізали мій вогонь на тисячі кілометрів
Від ярмарку в центрі Києва,
Де ці кілька глечиків —
Хтозна, якби трохи раніше, —
Могли б наповнитись копійками..
Але, видко, руки знали їм ціну,
Бо, здерті до крові,
Вирішили подарувати усі ті гроші
Снігові і вогню — єдиним свідкам,
Що мене таки спокусив ярмарок,
Але за такий дар, може, й простять..
Та, присівши далі від полум'я
Краєм ока зауважив,

WHITE HOT COALS

The bazaar tempted me.
The joy, the crowds—
Maybe I could sell something—
I have a couple of pots I haven't fired—
Tomorrow I'll get up early, fire them,
And sell them in the afternoon..
Heavy wet snow fell in the morning,
But it was too late to turn back..
So, I started dragging fallen trees into the ravine.
Even rotten, the blue-beech
Is hard inside, like a bone,
It hissed, smoked, I threw aside the saw
And bent over the fiery pit,
(Maybe it was an abandoned fox den):
The flames blazed, the coals turned white..
I could only tell time by the sun,
The snow did not stop,
From the bottom of the ravine, the snow and the wet logs
Made the market in the center of Kyiv
Seem a thousand kilometers away.
Where are those pots—
Who knows if I had started a little earlier—
Maybe they would be filled with coins by now..
These hands know their worth,
Look they're worn to the bone,
But they gave away all that money
To snow and fire—the only witnesses
To the fact that the bazaar tempted me,
Maybe now they will forgive me..
I squatted a little further from the flames
And noticed out of the corner of my eye,
That there were more witnesses—several listless,

Що з'явилися й інші свідки – декілька млявих,
Але таки зацікавлених мурашок –
Вони так само приглядались до вогню,
Сторожко обмацуючи нагріту землю..
Для них така подія теж могла бути
Неабияким досвідом в житті –
Отак, блукаючи якось
Коло Дальніх лаврськуих печер,
Надибав у кропиві кістку,
Трохи більшу за людську, і в її порожнині
Ворушився клубок рудух мурашок..
Отже, сама доля шле мені покупців –
Ну що ж, дивіться – робота вже готова –
Обвуленим дрючком розгрібаю жар..
Більша грудка – глечик,
Він – це людина і одночасно її дім.
На очах міниться її шкіра –
Ця мить в житті найкраща,
Цвітне рум'янець на щоках..
Та от пробігають перші тіні –
Тонко натягнута шкіра тримає ще жар..
..А тепер ми з вами раптом опиняємось
Всередині дуже хитрого сплетіння:
Згори суцільний сніг, а спиною чорні стовбури,
Лице в сажі, долоні так само,
Під ногами кваша зі снігу й попелу,
А під цим усім трохи нагріта зверху земля..
З такої пастики до ночі не виплутатись..
А тепер дивіться, що роблю:
Поки ще не зовсім потьмянів жар –
Беру дрючок і з усієї сили руйную
Навислий над випаленою ямою земляний дах –
Землю до землі!
Так одним ударом страшної лапи
Ведмідь при кінці зими обвалює

But still interested ants—
They also observed the fire,
Carefully feeling the heated earth..
This event could be
A life changing experience for them—
Once wandering around
The farthest grounds of the Lavra Monastery,
I found a bone in the nettles,
It was a little larger than human, and
A mass of red ants moved in its hollow.
It was a sign—fate is sending me buyers—
Well, look—the work is done—
I stirred the coals with a charred stick..
The bigger lump—was the pitcher,
The container and the contained.
Its skin changes in front of your eyes—
This is the most beautiful moment in life,
The cheeks grow rosy..
But here come the first shadows—
The stretched skin still white holds the heat
..And suddenly we find ourselves
Inside of a very tricky web:
Heavy snow above, dark tree trunks below,
Face covered in soot, as well as the hands,
A mix of ash and snow underfoot.
And underneath, the earth heated on the surface..
There's no escape from this trap..
So, what do I do:
Before the coals cool—
I take the stick and with all my might whack
The earth hanging over the burnt pit—
Earth to earth!
So, with one blow of his might paw
The bear wrecks his den,
His long warm dream

Свій барліг з усім його теплим сном,
Чесно зароблениим безконечними пошуками
І самітництвом..
Чи не здалось вам звідти, з пригрітої землі,
Отаким нетерплячим звіром на снігу?..
Чи ти, свідку, чекаєш, поки не впаду,
Щоб нарешті повідомити всіх,
Що мене таки спокусив ярмарок,
Але я не встиг, а що зміг – зруйнував
І загріб жар?..

And solitude..
Such an impatient beast on the snow..
Is that what you, crawling on the hot earth, think?
Are you waiting to see me fall,
So you can finally tell everyone,
That the bazaar tempted me,
But I didn't finish in time, so I wrecked what I made
And then buried the white hot coals?..

МАРТИН

В той день на ставах я бачив мертвого мартина.
Він погойдувався на воді коло самого берега,
Голова під крилом, ніби задрімав..
На білому причепуреному пір'ї ще не підсохла роса..
З дамби видно було безконечну воду, хмари,
Далі поле, ліс, а під ним темніла хата,
Де вже давно ніхто не жив..
Поле перетинав насип з дробленого каменю –
Колись до війни тут бігла колія
Зі Станіслава через Хриплин на Бучач,
Тепер порослий пирієм насип одним кінцем
Впирався в розібраний Залізний міст,
А другий, той що на Хриплин,
Губився в кущах глоду і терну..
Якби подивитися на нього згори
Чи не виглядав би звідти Змієвим валом
Чи Великим курганом Вужа?..
Але людині хіба не дано розпізнати не більше,
Ніж те, що вона годна сама переступити,
І то коли вона ще сильна і має твердий крок?..
Поле з лісом об'єднувала покинута хата..
Такої темної, ніби підплилої кров'ю цегли,
Ще, здається, не бачив.. може, тому що вона
Стояла під лісом? дах ще цілий,
Лише двері вивалені..
Зрештою, це могла бути нічна буря..
Але дивно – там, де спала колись жінка
(Кажуть, її чоловік щось зробив з собою) –
Сушиться сіно, натовкане аж під стелю..
Ану, хто тут, чи ти звір, чи хто – виходь!
Тихо.. і раптом з-під даху вислизає ластівка..
Так це ти тут тепер живеш..

SEAGULL

That day I saw a dead seagull on the pond.
It floated on the water near the shore,
Head tucked under its wing, as if it had just fallen asleep..
Dew on its beautiful white feathers..
Standing on the dam, I saw endless water and clouds.
Beyond the fields, at the edge of the forest stood a dark house.
No one had lived there in a long time..
The field was sliced in half by a mound of crushed rock—
Before the war a railroad ran there
From Stanislav, through Khryplyn to Buchach,
One end of the mound, now overgrown with wild grass,
Led up to the dismantled Iron Bridge
And the other, heading to Khryplyn,
Disappeared into hawthorn and thorn bushes..
If you could see it from above—
It probably would look like the Serpent's Wall[1]
Or the Great Serpent's Mound?..
But people only see it as
Something that they can step over,
If they are strong and their steps sturdy..
The abandoned home unites the field and the forest..
I had never seen such dark bricks, they seemed blood soaked,
Maybe it was because the house stood near the forest?
The roof was all there,
But the door had fallen in..
It could have happened during a storm at night..
But it was strange that where the woman once slept
(They say her husband did away with himself)—
Hay was piled up to the ceiling..
Whoever you are, man or beast, or whatever—come out!

---

[1] Serpent's Walls are ancient defensive earthworks, the remnants today stretch for
600 miles through central Ukraine.

Сама тікаєш на сонце, а своє сіно там лишила..
Віднаджуєш мене від нього..
Багато ж ти накосила, згромадила..
Правда, менше і не могло бути –
Бач, як розрахувала – щоб аж під саму стелю –
Витягувати зі стін затхлий дух людського житла..
Ти ж не вариш собі бульбу на обід
Чи трохи кулеші на сніданок?..
Хочеться вірити, що не ти, як то буває на самоті,
Жбурнула покривлену алюмінієву миску в кут –
А далі одним ударом розвалила почорнілий комин..
Чи й твої гострі крила в сажі?..
Я цілком випадково сюди забрів,
Мені таки не варто було втручатися у твій простір,
Так важко відвойований.. він мене розриває..
Ця темна, ніби підпливла кров'ю цегла спокушує,
Але ж це не людський дім..
Давно, коли я ще нічого на бачив,
На нашу річку під фабрикою
Звідкись заблукав мартин –
Він пролетів низьким коридором під деревами
І знов розвернувсь, і знов пролетів –
Звичайно, він помились, бо така ріка нічого
Йому не могла дати..
Того, що там він хотів знайти..
Його розпростері крила торкалися
Відразу обох берегів..
Ясно, він не міг цього нікому вибачити –
І своїм білим серед ночі польотом
Висушив її до дна..
Але ж я там жив, над тою вузькою річкою,
Затиснутою з одного боку фабрикою..
Тісно, справді..
Але.. чи можна сказати,
Що і мені вона нічого не дала?..

Silence.. and suddenly a swallow flew out..
Oh, so you live here now..
You escape towards the sun, and leave your hay behind..
You're trying to lead me away from it..
You mowed and gathered so much hay..
Less would not do—
I see, you made sure it would reach all the way to the ceiling—
To absorb the musty smell of humans..
You don't cook potatoes for lunch
Or porridge for breakfast?..
I don't believe it was you who tossed that bent aluminum bowl
Into the corner out of loneliness—
Or knocked down the dark chimney with one blow..
Or are your sharp wings covered in soot?..
I came here accidentally,
I shouldn't have intruded into your space,
So hard won.. it tears me up..
This dark, seemingly blood-soaked brick, is so tempting.
But this is not a human home..
Long ago, before I understood things,
A seagull lost its way
And came to our stream near the factory—
It flew through the narrow corridor formed by the trees
Then turned and flew back again—
It had made a mistake, this little stream
Could never give it anything
It would have wanted..
Its outstretched wings touched
Both banks at once..
It could not forgive this—
So its white flight in the middle of the night
Made the stream dry up..
But I lived there, on that narrow stream,
That was tightly pressed on one side
By the factory..
Can I say
It never gave me anything?..

ХЛОПЕЦЬ

Я зустрів його далеко за Тисменицею
На полі під лісом, де Стримба набагато дикіша,
І видно відразу, що це гірська річка,
Хоч мусить бігти по рівнині..
Мене здивувало, що він тут сам,
Ніде жодної душі,
А в такому віці, десь під шістнадцять,
Хлопці бігають табунами літом..
Присівши біля берега, по кістки у воді,
Дивився собі під ноги на щось блискучо-біле..
– Ну що, є риба? – спитав просто так..
– Нема, лише ця одна, плотиця.. я її видер
Під отим-во корчем, а тепер йду додому,
І хочу її випустити..
Трохи далі лежала повалена верба,
І там вже було глибоко –
Там треба було пірнути,
Аби запхати руки
Під стовбур столітнього дерева,
Обсмоктаного холодною течією,
З високо піднятим над водою
Одним-єдиним голим суком –
Здавалось, велетень-плавець
На мить занурив голову,
Перевернувся на бік
І викинув над собою правицю,
Але чомусь голова так і лишилась затоплена,
А рука і досі благає рятунку..
– Я пішов нурка і витягнув її звідти,
А вона тепер не може плисти..
І він погладив по синюватому хребті плотицю,
Яка ніби вигрівалась на сонці при березі,

BOY

I met him just outside the town of Tysmenytsia
In a field near the forest, where the Strymba River looks wilder,
And you can see it's really a mountain creek,
That has been forced to flow through the lowlands..
I was surprised to find him alone,
Not a living soul around,
Usually at that age, around sixteen,
Boys run in packs during the summer..
He was staring at his feet, squatting near the banks,
Ankle deep in the water when something white flashed..
"There's fish here?"—I asked him..
"No, there's only one carp, I pulled her out
From under the tree that fell into the river,
Now I'm going home and want to let her go.."
A little further upstream where the water's deep,
Lay a willow trunk—
You would have had to dive into the water
To get your hands under
The trunk of that hundred year old tree,
Lapped by the cool stream,
One naked branch
Stuck out of the water—
Like the right arm
Of some giant
Swimming on his side
In the river,
For some reason he keeps his head underwater,
While his arm reaches out for help..
"I dove down and pulled the fish out," the boy said,
"But now she can't swim.."
He stroked the bluish spine,
As she warmed herself in the sun near the banks,

Лежачи на боці, розморено здвигаючи
Яскравими пірцями..
Її гаряча, сповнена любові, оболонка ока
Дивилась на хлопця,
Низько похиленого над водою –
І він, здається, теж більше нікого не помічав..
Його рука бавилася з нею..
І плотиця ніби й хоче
Вже відплисти на більшу воду,
Та не наважується,
І знову тягнеться до пестливої руки..
– Нічого, – він вибачливо звів на мене очі, –
– Я зачекаю, поки вона відійде,
І аж тоді піду додому..
Я там його лишив. Оглянувшись здалеку,
Знов побачив самотню зігнену фігурку..
Це ж і я колись нишпорив по глибоких норах,
Звідки часом могла вислизнути гадюка..
А він якийсь нетутешній –
Худий, засмаглий.. синюваті білки
Ледь скошених очей..
Такі уста подобаються дівчатам..
Де він тепер?..

Lying on her side, she tiredly flicked
Her bright fins..
Her warm filmy eyes, lovingly,
Watched the boy
Bent over the water—
He didn't notice anything else..
As he played with her..
The fish wanted to swim off
Into the deeper water,
But was afraid
And returned to the boy's hand..
"It's no trouble," he looked up with his kind eyes,
"I will wait till she swims off
And then I'll go home."
I left him there. When I looked back again
I saw his lone figure bent over the water..
Once, I too explored deep burrows,
But sometimes a snake would crawl out..
The boy was a bit otherworldly—
Thin, tanned, a hint of blue in the whites of his eyes
Slightly cross eyed..
Girls like lips like his..
I wonder where he is today?..

ДНІСТЕР

from DNISTER

ДНІСТЕР

1

Мерехтять білі метелики
Над горбами червоної конюшини..
Чи це вчулось овече блеяння?..
Я лежу впоперек дороги, головою в конюшині,
І розглядаю на долоні
Крем'яну сокирку з просвердленим отвором..
Вгорі пропливають три чаплі –
З боків звичайні, попелясті,
А посередині біла-біла,
Ніби охороняють її, щоб ніхто
Не захляпав кров'ю її рідкісне пір'я..
Але, мабуть, вже недалеко вода,
Бо розлітаються кожна на свій обрій..
І вже скоро побачу те, що й вони в долині –
Але не точним пташиним оком, –
А зіницею з розтріснутими капілярами,
Крізь червоний туман понад горбами,
Через крем'яну сокиру, в її отвір..

DNISTER RIVER

1

White moths shimmer
Over hills of red clover..
Did I just hear a sheep?..
I lie with my head in the clover,
And examine a flint axe
With a hole bored through it..
Three herons fly overhead
A snow-white one in the center
And two grey ones on each side,
As if guarding her, so no one
Splatters her rare plumage with blood..
There must be water nearby
Because each bird heads downward..
Soon I'll see them in the valley—
Not from a bird's eye view—
But through blood shot eyes,
Through the red mist of the clover-covered hills,
Through the hole in the axe made of flint..

2

Корова стояла коло самої води
І невидющими очима вглядалась
В рідке каламутне шкло..
Далеко-далеко понад низьким берегом,
Порослим кущами бурого кінського щавлю
На паромі відпливали в тумані
її далекі сестри..
Підійшла жінка, відтягає корову від води..
Босі, подряпані старі ноги..
Я показав рукою на другий берег —
Його вже не було видно в темряві:
— А що там за село на тому боці?
— Не знаю.. я там ніколи не була..

2

A cow stands near the water
Staring with its uncomprehending eyes
Into the glassy, muddy flow..
Far-far away past the river bank
Overgrown with brown sorrel,
Her distant sisters float off on a barge
Into the mist..
A woman approaches and pulls the cow away from the water..
Her feet are bare, scratched and old..
I point to the other bank—
No longer visible in the dark:
"What's the village on the other side?"
"I don't know.. I've never been there.."

3

Мене збудили поштовхи.. я хилився надвір,
У холод, крізь розхитану стіну вагона..
Відразу за вікном у мряці тремтів
Присохлий листок кукурудзи.. по радіо схлипувала
Безконечна мелодія пісної мамалиґи..
Далі простягалась пустеля,
Зрідка оживлена плямкою корови..
Стікали краплі брудним склом..
Вже не видно було нічого.. лише чути,
Як тріщить хребет поїзда..
Як мене вигинає, крутить
Його млява, недалека тінь..
Прощай.. я не побачу тебе ніколи..

3

Sharp shoves wake me.. I press against
The cold, shaky walls of the rail car..
In the mist just outside the window
A dry corn stalk trembles.. a sappy endless melody
Whines on the radio..
A wasteland stretches beyond..
Rarely enlivened by dark specks that might be cows..
Drops of water slide down the dirty glass..
I see nothing else.. but hear
The spine of the train screech..
As it bends, twisting me
In its pale, blurry shadow..
Farewell.. I will never see you again..

COH

from DREAM

СОН

1

річка.. камінь..
мати миє посуд..
я з рушником за спиною –
витираю насухо..
кістки риби викидаються на дно..
хребет біліє на дні..
дрібні рибки шастають довкола..
мати, розвіявши волосся, обертається..
в чистім повітрі блищать її очі..
киває на рибок –
заметушились придкіш,
визбирують рештки обіду..
літо.. вечір..
уста в ожині..
пальці поколено, та крові не видно..
на низанці два окуні,
ледь поблідлі від давньої смерті..
– дорога.. де ти?.. твої пальці.. обличчя..
– подай трохи хліба, он там
ти сіла біля нього..
вже клює? невже клює?..
підкинь кілька крихт –
он туди, бач? – поплавок за осокою..

DREAM

1

river.. rock..
mother washes dishes..
I stand behind her with a towel—
drying them..
fish bones sink to the bottom..
a spine glows white from below..
tiny fish dart around..
mother, tossing her hair, turns..
her eyes shine in the crisp air..
she points to the fish—
they scurry,
picking at the leftovers..
summer.. evening..
lips stained with blackberries..
fingers pricked, but not bloody..
two perch hang on a string,
so pale, they've been dead a long time..
"where are you, my heart?. your fingers.. face.."
"pass the bread, over there"
you sat down..
"are the fish biting? really biting?..
throw a couple of crumbs—
over there, past the aspen, see the cork bob?.."

2

..та вагітна щука під мостом..
як топтали воду..
аж за годину спливла..
вона чимось пахла..
в мене закрутилась голова..
я пішов танцювати..
потім знов пішов танцювати..
тоді я добре танцював..
звідки я знав, що так скінчиться?
почали прискіпуватись,
нібито я піймав її голіруч..
підійшов один і спитав,
за що його колись вдарив каменем між очі?..
я сказав: ви здорово відплатили! –
я був такий довірливий,
а ви заманили до річки:
ніби там на отій низенькій вербі
дупло одуда..
почав видряпуватись, а ви зіштовхнули у воду!
якраз був листопад –
я вже пускав бульки в довгій шубі
з собачих і овечих клаптів..
добре – надбігли сусіди і
витягли ще живого!..

2

.. we splashed through the water
under the bridge and an hour later..
a pregnant pike floated down..
she smelled..
my head spun..
I started to dance..
then I danced again..
I was a good dancer then..
how could I have known how it would end?
they accused me..
of catching her with my hands..
then someone said
once I'd hit him with a stone right between the eyes..
I said: "well, you got me back good
I was so trusting,
you enticed me to the river:
saying that there was a kingfisher nest
in the willow tree near the water..
I started to climb up, and you pushed me into the river!
it was November—
I was in a long coat made of scraps of dog fur and sheep,
soon you could see bubbles rise..
good thing the neighbors came and
dragged me out barely alive!.."

3

..посидь отут на межі.. почекай..

я викопаю тобі хруща..

почекай, почекай.. я викопаю тобі хруща –

ти у вологій долоні

зробиш собі радіо під вухом..

я не знав, що таке хрущ..

було холодно.. цвіли нарцизи.. я чекав..

..того вечора їй стало сімдесят..

ми ввійшли до неї, обнявшись..

розглянувсь по хаті.. посуд не митий..

– нічого не варила..

не знаю і чим тебе частувати.. –

вона вибігла і тут же вбігла:

– заплющ очі – вгадай!

– ти хочеш мене почастувати?..

– так-так.. розплющ око –

ось – нарциз.

я його зірвала з інеєм ще в суботу..

думала – приїдеш в суботу..

ліжко під одхиленим вікном..

ранком захрипло: весна-а..

3

..sit here on the edge.. wait..
I will dig up a may bug..
wait, wait.. I will dig up a may bug just for you—
you can hold it to your ear, a radio
in your sweaty palm..
I did not know what a may bug was..
it was cold.. a narcissus bloomed.. I waited..
..that evening she turned seventy..
we walked to her house and embraced her..
I looked around.. the dishes weren't washed..
"I haven't made anything..
don't know what to put on the table.."
she ran out and then ran right back in:
"close your eyes—guess!"
"is it a treat?"
"yes-yes.. open your eyes
Here it is—a narcissus..
I picked it on Saturday all covered with frost..
I thought you were coming on Saturday.."
the bed under the open window..
in the morning squeaked: spring-ring..

4

..ми з батьком знов не спали —
хтось видовбував молоду картоплю
батькове збліддле чоло..
він згоряв на моїх очах..
— дивись.. вона.. як вагітна..
притиснула картоплину до грудей.. співає..
опускається до річки.. біжить!..
добре вглядайсь:
ті темні кола під очима..
той сухорлявий палець на вустах.. —
то ж твоя мати..

4

..father and I could not sleep again—
someone was digging up the new potatoes..
father's forehead was pale..
he was burning up before my eyes..
"look.. she looks.. pregnant..
holding a potato to her breast.. she sings..
goes down to the river.. and runs!..
take a good look:
those dark circles under her eyes..
that thin finger held to her lips..—
she's your mother.."

5

..такий ранковий гай – навіть піднесеш долоні!..
хтось і вибіг – то я? –
як тут в тебе? – не підрізати кілька опеньків? –
швидше кажи!
– я тут до ранку – ранком опаду..
і не пустив коріння, почув – ти тут..
– хоч присяду.. хоч кину стебло пахучої осоки –
може, пальці твої поріднаться – ти і вона..
я ж вибіг по одній росі –
над рікою ніби хтось співає:
«..радуйсь, ріко.. і ти, нещасливцю –
ти піймав одну з нас.. вітаєм!..»
там зачерпнув верхоплавку:
– скажи, що це все значить?!
вона злякано метнулась між пальців:
– ну хіба ти не знаєш?.. прощання..
– як?!..
– і ти тут?
бачу, не загоїлось вухо..
бач, коли проштрикнула мочки –
ти була не така.. тепер ні сережок..
тут поруччя розхитане – міст так високо!..
– я тебе не злякала тоді
на галяві в тіні? – ти спав..
я підкралась близько-близько..
твоє дихання..
я шепнула – долоня до вуст –
ти в сні відповів..

5

..what a beautiful morning among the trees—just throw your
     hands in the air!..
          someone ran out—is that me?
"so,—any good mushrooms around here?
tell me, come on!"
"I'll be here till dawn, in the morning I'll be gone..
didn't put down any roots, but I sensed you'd be here.."
"just let me sit.. on this fragrant grass—
maybe your fingers will become familiar—yours and hers"
I ran through the morning dew—
it seemed someone was singing by the river:
"rejoice, river.. and you sad young man—
you caught one of us.. congratulations!"
hooked a small fish:
"tell me what does it all mean?!"
frightened, she quickly looked between my fingers:
"don't you know?.. parting.."
"what?!"
"and you're here..
I can see your ear hasn't healed..
see, you were not like this
when you pierced your ears.. now, no earrings.."
the railing is shaky—and the bridge is so high!..
"did I frighten you
when you slept?.. in the shadow of the tree..
I crept up close-close..
your breath..
cupping my hand to my lips—I whispered—
you answered in your dream.."

6

..бім.. бім.. скапують краплі під міст..
згадую кучері дівчини..
як торкнулась мокрою рукою —
із криком полетіли униз!..
та найвеселіше, як на міст
видряпувавсь сам шекспір —
ми чіпляли йому руду бороду —
він починав:
— я тільки поет! — «сон літньої ночі!» —
перший найкращий і останній мій твір!..
ми сердились:
— ти наш сон.. сон нашої ночі! —
ти не розумієш трагічності наших літ!..
у воді крадькома торкались вуст, грудей..
міст темнів — ми потискали руки:
— добраніч, шекспіре..
ми не впізнали тебе..
— добраніч.. добраніч.. добраніч..
ви не впізнали? — так, це я..

6

..drip .. drip.. the drops fall off the bridge..
I remember the curls in her hair..
she touched me with her wet hand—
we jump down shrieking!..
but it's most fun when Shakespeare himself
climbs up on the bridge—
we pin a red beard on him—
and he starts:
"I am only a poet!—midsummer night's dream
is my first best and last work!"
we get angry:
"you are our dream.. our night's dream!—
you do not understand our tragedies today!"
in the water on the sly we touch lips, breasts..
the bridge darkens—
we shake hands:
"goodnight, Shakespeare.."
"goodnight.. goodnight.. goodnight..
you did not recognize me?—well, it's me.."

3 ADAMO ET DIANA

from ADAMO ET DIANA

1 DE LUMINIS

У Кракові на Плянтах, недалеко від Вавеля під старими плакучими вербами ховається археологічний музей.. В одній його залі посередині стоїть кам'яний стовп Світовид. Там він виринає завжди якось несподівано з напівтемряви, холодний, ніби і досі його обмивають темні, студені води Збруча.. А за стіною у світлішій залі єгипетські саркофаги — яскраві, золотаво-червонясті дерев'яні личини кількох пізніх фараонів. Їхніх мумій усередині вже немає.. Зате є мумія сокола, і я завмирав над нею годинами.. Хоч що там побачиш?.. Може, усередині якась деревинка, сліпа, завинута туго у полотняну ряднину?.. Про що я думав тоді, низько похилившись над продовгуватим чистим сповитком?.. Що часом і я таки колись був вільним? Часом, дуже рідко, але таки вільним?.. Чи про те, що і цей сповитий стовпчик, і той кам'яний стовп Світовид за стіною у темнішій залі були разом різними відтинками єдиного сонячного стовпа?.. Променя з небесного сліпучого ока, що пронизує усе до найглибших глибин, як би не ховався у місячнім дзеркалі?.. Чи, може, думав, що над королівським Вавелем зовсім поруч зараз у небі незрушно ширяє вічна варта кількох таких самих соколів-голуб'ятників і невтомним вигостреним оком озирають усе, що діється тут, набагато нижче, щоб жоден заблуканий голуб не заплямив своїм послідом цю королівську твердиню?.. Минають дні і ночі, минають століття, міняється варта в один і той же час, навчена пильнувати земну твердиню з неба..

1 DE LUMINIS (About Light)

In Krakow, not far from Wawel Castle, an archeological museum hides under the old weeping willows of Plantes Park.. In the center of an exhibition hall stands a stone pillar called *Svitovyd* [1] (World-Seer). It appears unexpectedly out of the shadows, cool, as if it were still in the dark waters of the Zbruch River.. Next, in a much brighter room there are Egyptian sarcophagi, bright golden-red wooden caskets that once held various pharaohs. Their mummies are no longer inside.. But there is a mummy of a falcon, and I hovered over it for several hours.. What was there to see?.. Inside maybe there's just a little stump, blind, thickly wrapped in linen?.. What was I thinking about as I bent over the long swaddling?.. Maybe that once I too was free? Long ago, and only for little while, but nonetheless free?.. Or was I thinking that this swaddled little stump and the Svitovyd pillar behind the wall in the dark room were different aspects of the same shaft of light?.. Were they the rays from heaven's dazzling eye which penetrate everything down to the most profound depths, and even behind the mirror of the moon you can't hide from them?... Or maybe I was thinking about the eternal guard of young falcons hovering in the sky over the royal Wawel Castle.. Their tireless clear-sighted eyes see all that happens here, way down below, making sure that even the shadow of a stray pigeon doesn't darken the royal stronghold.. Days and nights pass, centuries pass, the eternal guard from the heavens continues to change, trained to protect this citadel on earth..

---

[1] A stone statue of an ancient Slavic god commonly believed to be the god of war. It was discovered in 1848 in the Zbruch River. Erected in the 9th century, it was probably thrown into the river after the area accepted Christianity. At the top of the pillar are four faces each set in a different direction. On the sides are three layers of images that illustrate mythological beliefs of the time: the heavens with the gods living in them, the Earth inhabited by people, and the underworld dominated by evil forces. Since 1851 the idol has been in the Krakow Archaeological Museum.

ON POETRY, TRANSLATION, AND THEATRE

Virlana Tkacz

I LOVE POETRY, my house is full of poetry books. But, I believe great poetry is meant to be heard out loud, and the stage is the best place for it. Yara Arts Group, which I direct, creates theatre pieces using poetry. So that I could include Ukrainian poems in our theatre productions, I started working on translations with American poet Wanda Phipps.

I can only translate poems that speak to me. I try to capture the poem as I hear it in English by quickly jotting down a draft. Then I go back, look up words, and consult with the poet. Most importantly, I read the poem out loud with Wanda Phipps. Then she reads it to me, and we shift and correct words, constantly reading the poem out loud until it sounds just right in English. That is how we create our translations.

It is ten times harder for me to correct someone else's translation than to create one myself. I can't hear the voice in someone else's draft. Also, I think each translation must speak to its intended audience. The audiences for our translations include the young Americans who are Yara artists, their friends, and the New York theatre-goers who come to our shows.

I am not interested in talk theatre, where characters sit and complain about their families. I want a theatre that opens new worlds for me, one that lets me see and experience things I never knew existed. The distilled language and imagery of poetry suggest openings into spaces where creativity hovers. Oleh Lysheha writes such poetry.

Oleh Lysheha

IN 1990, I MET MYKOLA RIABCHUK at Veselka Restaurant in New York City. He was one of the first people I met from Soviet Ukraine who was roughly my age. Previously, visiting "young poets" from

Ukraine were my parents' age. Riabchuk told me that there was a new generation of poets in Ukraine. He had a stack of manuscripts and an anthology he had just put together with Ihor Rymaruk called *Visimdesiatnyky* (The Generation of the 1980s). The book included forty new poets and was published by the Canadian Institute of Ukrainian Studies in Edmonton. He gave me a copy.

I went home and started reading. I loved the poems by Oksana Zabuzhko, Attila Mohylny and Victor Neborak. But, when I read Oleh Lysheha's "Song 212," I thought I heard the young urban beat of Ukraine I had been searching for. I rushed around trying to find a copy of his book. Bohdan Boychuk lent me a Xerox of Lysheha's *Great Bridge,* and I sank into a world where Paleolithic horses spoke from cave walls and old illiterate Hutsul women turn out to be the true judges and guardians of Franko's spirit. I was mesmerized. This was like nothing else I had ever read.

Wanda Phipps, who translates with me, also liked the Lysheha texts, so we set to work. Soon, several poems by Oleh Lysheha became staples at Yara Arts Group Poetry Events, where our actors read the works bilingually, intertwining the original and our English translation.

I particularly liked "Mountain" which delved into an archaic past but ended facing the future: "Somewhere above we heard voices.. / Children shouting into the heavens.." We included this piece in Yara's Theatre Workshops at Harvard in July 1991. Yuri Shevchuk read it as part of our "Radio Eternity: Ukrainian Poetry from the 1920s and 1990s."

For eleven years I conducted theatre workshops for the Ukrainian Summer School at Harvard. Every spring I would read the new poetry published in Ukrainian journals and make copies of the poems I liked. When the pile grew thick enough, I would read through the poems again, looking for a theme. This would become the theme of the production I staged with the students using the poems as text.

Svitlana Matviyenko who attended Yara's last Theatre Workshop at Harvard in 1998, best described our way of work:

126

Virlana Tkacz's method and practice depends on the de(con)struction of a poem. That is, in the beginning the text is divided into tiny fragments of a line or two, which are parceled out. Then we tried to find related fragments. These lines were then given to a single actor. And then—the parceled-out text is reunited during the flow of the stage action. It was fascinating, using this method, to stumble upon inner monologues, dialogues or even poly-logues. A polyphony (almost straight from Bakhtin) of various voices, was "read" (or rather was "heard") in Oksana Zabuzhko's poem.

Perhaps we were engaged in the creation of new texts, or perhaps yet another interpretation—but we were free in our behavior. It was important to play, to pronounce the words out loud.

—*"Virlana Tkacz and Her Theatre" by Svitlana Matvienko, Informatsinyi Biuleten, Kyiv, November 1998.*

Oleh Lysheha's poems often became a part of these workshop productions.

SWAN

In the spring of 1993, Wanda and I met Oleh Lysheha in person for the first time. We were in Kyiv rehearsing Yara's *Blind Sight* and a mutual friend brought him to a party. Oleh then told me that he had written some longer poems. The following year, the Ukrainian journal *Suchasnist* published these poems. Lysheha's long poem "Swan" cast a spell on me. I was totally taken with the idea of transformation and our relationship to the animal spirit within us. That summer I worked with Oleh Drach, an actor from the Lviv Young Theatre, trying to imagine the six-page poem as a theatre piece. In July 1995, we performed our first attempt at Yara's Theatre Workshop—*Oceanic Consciousness: Growing Fangs, Tails and Wings.*

As soon as Wanda and I translated "Swan," I started to include parts of our translation in Yara's new theatre production *Wayward Wind.* This show about nomads in the steppes and online, would eventually become *Virtual Souls,* our first collaborative project with the Buryat National Theatre in Siberia.

My fascination with Lysheha's poem led me to look for mythical material on swans. The most fascinating swan stories were Buryat. "The swan is our mother and the birch—our family tree," say the old Buryats. The Buryats live in Siberia in the area around Lake Baikal. Buryatia has been part of the Russian Empire since the 17th century and today it is a republic within the Russian Federation. The Buryat chronicles begin with a legend about a hunter who sees wild swans take off their swan dresses and turn into beautiful girls. While the girls are swimming in Lake Baikal, he steals one of the swan dresses. Startled, most of the swans fly off, leaving one behind to plead with the hunter to give back her dress. We included this legend in *Virtual Souls,* and Yara was invited to the Buryat National Theatre to work on the project.

That summer, I flew to Siberia with Tom Lee, a Yara actor, to work with the Buryat artists. Three young artists—Sayan and Erzhena Zhambalov, plus Erdeny Zhaltsanov—met us. At first, we struggled to communicate through an interpreter, but I soon realized they could understand me if I spoke Ukrainian slowly. Tom and I acted out the story of our play for our three colleagues. Once we managed to explain what the internet was (this was 1996) and the rather incredible story of how we found The Buryat chronicles in the New York Public Library, the sections of Lysheha's "Swan" that we had included in the text seemed an obvious fit.

The mythic sections of our production took place on Lake Baikal, and I had dreamt of rehearsing our piece there. When the rest of the Yara artists arrived, we piled into a tiny bus and left for what the Buryats call the "sacred sea." As the women in the cast "flew" on the shore of Baikal, we realized our deep connection to this huge body of pristine water. Eventually, our play would end with a scene where the entire cast moved slowly back into this primordial element.

On the way back from the Baikal, our bus had a flat tire on top of a mountain. Our bus driver actually managed to lift the bus without a jack, while Yara's designer Watoku Ueno figured out how to fix the flat using only my Swiss Army knife. As we stood around the bus on a tiny road in the freezing night, Tom Lee and Andrew Pang suddenly started performing a section of Lysheha's "Swan" to the moon:

> Moon, come here..
> I come out from under the pines—you're hiding..
> I go back under the pines—you shine..
> I start running—you're at my back..
> I stop—you're gone..
> Only dark pines..
> I hide behind a pine—and you come out..
> I come out—you're not there..
> Not there..
> Not there..
> There..
> Not there..
> There.. not there..
> I can't move that fast..
> Wait.. I want to
> Stand in your light..

Lysheha must have been writing about this very moon and this very spot. I learned about Lysheha's connection to Buryatia only on the day I was leaving for Siberia. Serhiy Proskurnia, who had produced our shows in Kyiv, arrived in New York that morning and we talked as I tried to pack. At one point, I asked him if he thought I was crazy for going off to Ulan Ude. "No," he replied, "it makes perfect sense. After all, Lysheha had been there and was very influenced by the art and philosophy." I couldn't believe my ears. Lysheha had been to Buryatia? "Yes," Serhiy answered, "didn't you know that?" "No, during my research I happened upon the

Buryat material." At first, Serhiy thought I was kidding. Then he realized that I had indeed made this connection on my own. He told me what he knew. In the 1970s, Oleh Lysheha was involved with a college literary magazine called *Skrynia* (*The Chest*) that published translations of Western modernist poets such as Ezra Pound. During the purges of 1972, the police decided that this was a nationalist publication, and Lysheha was expelled from Lviv State University. He was forced into the Soviet Army and sent to Buryatia. I don't think the actors knew about Lysheha's stay in Buryatia, but obviously, they too felt a deep connection in this poem as we stood there shivering in the Siberian night.

We performed *Virtual Souls* at the Buryat National Theatre in English and in Buryat in September 1996. That winter, we premiered the show with our Buryat colleagues at La MaMa in Manhattan. In April 1997, we brought the show to Kyiv where it was part of the Berezillia Theatre Festival.

In the winter of 1998, I worked on a new piece with artists from the Buryat National Theatre. It was called *Flight* and was based on stories and songs we collected the previous summer in Siberia. Again, I included sections of Oleh Lysheha's "Swan." This time they served as texts for songs composed by Genji Ito. Lysheha was a Fulbright scholar in Pennsylvania that year and came to New York to see the workshop of our show. We convinced him to stay long enough for us to arrange for a reading of his poetry at the Mayana Gallery.

At the poetry event, Oleh read several of his recent poems, holding his Ukrainian-speaking audience rapt. One of my friends told me afterwards, "They're like great avant-garde films that tell a complicated story while allowing the shifting point of view to transform not only our view of the story, but also of the entire storytelling process."

Then Oleh Lysheha started reading my favorite poem, "Swan." After Oleh read the powerful ending, the audience sat hushed. Tom Lee got up and read our translation of "Swan." I had heard Tom read sections of this poem many times in rehearsal. I had even heard him recite pieces of it in the middle of the night on a dirt road in Siberia. But I hadn't heard anyone read the entire text recently. I was very moved experiencing all the twists and turns of a soul searching for transcendence in the difficult pettiness of what constituted life in Ukraine those days. Tom's interpretation was very different from Lysheha's cool delivery. We were all swept away. Afterwards, there was a lot of talk about poetry, readings, and the cultural adventures Lysheha had sent us all on.

Five years later, I staged the entire text of Oleh Lysheha's poem "Swan" at La MaMa E.T.C. with Andrew Colteaux. In the spring of 2003, I was in San Francisco visiting a friend and called Andrew who had been in several early Yara productions but had returned home to live in Marin County. He read the poem and agreed to work with me on the show in New York. We decided to keep it simple. Watoku Ueno, Yara's designer, is a minimalist. He created a wooden fence with a door, evoking the fences that line the back roads of Ukraine. I invited Paul Brantley, a cellist and composer, to create the music and perform it live on stage. As he reacted musically to Andrew's every move, Paul became both the cherry tree and the man dancing under it.

The other living presence in the poem was the bicyclist who Watoku first fashioned as a shadow puppet descending down from the heavens on a paper road. On stage, the bicyclist arrived as Soomi Kim, a Yara actor who was also a champion gymnast. Dressed exactly as Andrew, but half his size, she became his double, the spirit he struggles with.

Meredith Wright created the voice of the moon. Meredith had performed the section of the meeting with the swan as a song in *Flight of the White Bird.* Now as the moon, she was an observer, not an active participant. Meredith described her approach to the music:

> I decided an abstraction of the text would best support the performers. I chose a few select words and phrases and meditated on the melodies that I believed were already embodied within them. I experimented with the

manipulation of vowels and consonants to see how they resonated over the rich score of music and movement and text. The word "ashes," for example, demanded attention in the way the "shh" lingers when the word is said. This single word provided me with several melodic possibilities. A touching moment between the characters inspired a lullaby sung primarily on the sound "ooh." Then I added, "cling to me . . . I'll carry you," a paraphrase of Lysheha words. A whimsical refrain on the word "la" accompanied cellist Paul Brantley, and weaved in and out of the production. This process required the unraveling of words and phrases in a way that best explains the purpose of poetry. I believe poetry is essentially a deliberate linking of words and phrases used to evoke emotions. I responded with a song.

I asked Olga Shuhan, who worked on many Yara shows, to be the Ukrainian voice we heard in the show. At times, she sounded like an echo or a lingering question. Towards the end of the piece, she was the voice of the generous neighbor, who gives the main character three eggs and "a knowing look."

Andrea Odezynska filmed a swan in Brooklyn, which: "turned its head and disappeared.. Just as suddenly." At that moment in the show, Watoku had the massive looking wooden wall imperceptibly move away from us and Andrew stepped into the water after the swan. Leaning on small benches, Andrew and Soomi seemed to float on stage:

> It was only me and the swan
> Eyes wide open,
> Not bound by a bottom or a sky..

Soomi got up and held a finger to her lips, as Meredith sang, then she turned and disappeared behind the wooden door, where we had just seen the long neck of the swan.

Swan premiered at La MaMa E.T.C. June 12 - 29, 2003. Eva Yaa Asantewaa of the *Village Voice* wrote: "Soomi Kim and Andrew Colteaux's efficient yet expressive acting and imaginative movement, a simple set by Watoku Ueno, and spare, warm notes bowed and plucked from composer Paul Brantley's cello, the sole instrument played live—allowed true feeling to permeate the action."

Then in July, we performed *Swan* at Harvard University. Critic Dzvinka Matiash saw our show at Harvard and wrote:

> The production of *Swan* is a virtuoso translation of Lysheha's text—it is not simply a literary translation into English, but rather a translation of poetry into the languages of music, light, image, movement of the human body, human voice (that can sound sharp, hoarse, strained, tired, lonely), and of course, stage space. The result is polyphonic; various voices are united so that each has its place and is heard . . . Cellist (Paul Brantley), listens to the modulation of a soprano as pure as silver (Meredith Wright), he listens to the human voice (of Andrew Colteaux). The poetry interweaves with music, Ukrainian becomes an echo of the English, dance becomes an extension of the voice, and bodies continue to speak as the voice grows silent. What the voice cannot say, the man and woman say with their movements. This is what art should be like—in the glare of the stage lights you suddenly see the essence. But you can only catch a glimpse of it, just as you can only glimpse the swan in this show.
>
> —*Komentar, Kyiv, November 2003*

RAVEN

My adventure with Lysheha's "Raven" started dramatically. Oleh and I arranged to meet at noon in the main square of Lviv. Just as the bell above rang twelve, Lysheha stepped out of the bright sunlight next to a stone lion that guards the old city hall. He suggested a café and we carefully made our way over the snow-covered cobblestones to the other side of the old square lined with Baroque churches and Renaissance storefronts. We talked for several hours about his work and the translation of his poem "Raven" that I had recently completed with Wanda Phipps. He liked the translation and gave me permission to stage it.

I had come to Lviv with Andrew Colteaux, who had created the main character in *Swan*. On the train, we got to know Larysa Rusnak. I had met her at a singing workshop in Kyiv the previous fall and had seen her perform the part of Frida Kahlo in Franko Theatre's production *Two Indigo Flowers*. She is a fiery performer and one of my favorite actors in Kyiv. I was glad to hear she was interested in joining our workshop at the Pasika Theatre Center at the University of Kyiv-Mohyla Academy.

I also invited Mykola Shkaraban who appeared in Yara's first production in Ukraine. Mykola and Andrew had met in 1993 on Yara's third project, *Blind Sight*. That spring, Mykola became the first Ukrainian actor Yara brought to perform at La MaMa. He spoke English well, so the bilingual interweaving we do seemed natural to him. He also hung out with Andrew and their scenes in *Raven* reflected the depth of their friendship.

Victoria Shupikova performed Miss Julie in a wild production of the Strindberg play at Pasika. I loved her fierce commitment to the part and asked her to join our *Raven* workshop. She appeared as the student whitewashing the wall in the beginning and, later, as Ivan's wife—a ghost on live video who appears in the wilderness.

Design was a very important element in this show and in all shows based on poetry. Design brings the poetic images to life on the stage. Zhenya Kopiov is the resident light designer at the Kurbas Theatre Center in Kyiv, where I worked with him since 2004. I met Waldemart Klyuzko in 2010 when he helped us build the set for *Scythian Stones* at Gogolfest. I invited them to work with us as a team on *Raven*, and they have worked together ever since.

Waldemart has said:

> The design for the show was developed in rehearsal in collaboration with actors. When we first came into the space and the actors started reading the text, we tried to find elements they could use. I found a moving wall made of transparent plastic in a metal frame on wheels. At first, I taped paper pages to the plastic so we could see the projections. The next day, I bought a cheap wavy plastic used for insulation and covered the wall. This became our projection surface. As the moving screen spun, it reflected the projected image on the walls and throughout the space. We used this to create the wild chase in the wilderness. The interplay between Zhenya's lights and my projections allowed us to use the actors like shadow puppets. We discovered that if we projected an image from the front and lit the actor with a strong light from behind, their shadow formed a cutout of the projection.
>
> The most striking use of this discovery was in the final moments of the show. As Andrew reached towards Larysa, who was behind the screen, she turned from a lush embodiment of the wilderness into a raven that flew away as she moved in tandem with the screen.

That winter, Eva Salina Primack and Aurelia Shrenker who specialize in traditional music from the Republic of Georgia and the Balkans, worked with me on Yara's *Winter Sun*. At the time, they were interested in Appalachian ballads, so I asked them to record several songs for our production of *Raven*. I invited Ukrainian composer Alla Zahaykevych, who often combines traditional music with a live electronic score, to join our project. Eventually, we also included master bandura player Julian Kytasty who created an additional interesting layer in the music of our show.

We developed the basic idea of our theatre piece in Ukraine but premiered *Raven* in April 2011 at La MaMa Experimental Theatre in the East Village. The Ukrainian actors Larysa Rusnak, Mykola Shkaraban, and Victoria Shupikova could not travel to New York, but I knew wonderful Yara actors who could take up their parts and make them their own. The La MaMa production of *Raven* featured Yara actors, both old and new. Sean Eden had worked on Yara's first play in 1990 and traveled with us to Ukraine in 1991. Kat Yew had appeared in two Yara winter projects, while *Raven* was Maren Bush's first Yara production. I also asked Olga Shuhan to read some of the text in Ukrainian—making for a truly diverse Yara production.

Thanks to the projections by Waldemart Klyuzko and his New York counterpart, Mikhail Shraga, our simple set—with one movable screen—exploded with color and movement as the characters spun it, running through the forest in search of an invisible path. Both the audience and press were left breathless:

> *Raven* incites this ensemble to glorious flight. The path flown by *Raven* is, by turns, intoxicating in both its simplicity and complexity. I encourage you to follow where it leads.
>
> —*Amy Lee Pearsall for nytheatre.com.*

"This is a show you can and want to watch many times. Each time you discover something new, as I can testify." wrote Lydia Korsun in *Svoboda*, while lhor Slabicky called it "a magical event that captures you and does not let you go." Olena Jennings agreed in her review of the show for *The Ukrainian Weekly*, and praised Andrew Colteaux for his compelling performance. Yara's *Raven* was nominated for a New York Innovative Theatre Award.

In June, I was able to return to Kyiv with Andrew Colteaux to once again work with the Ukrainian artists. We performed *Raven* at Pasika from June 10 - 14, 2011. Kyiv's *KinoTeatr* journal wrote:

the most amazing thing about *Raven* is the magical and masterful way the poetic text has been transformed into stage reality . . . the show is an interesting and unforgettable adventure that is both intellectual and emotional.

After our shows in Kyiv, the company traveled to Lviv for performances at the Les Kurbas Theatre on June 22 - 23. Our projections demanded a lot of backstage space, but the Kurbas Theatre is a small jewel of a theatre and the largest space available is round. So, Zhenya and Waldemart had to work extra hard, but, ultimately, came up with some very creative solutions.

The shows sold out days ahead, and the Lviv audiences loved the production. The critic for Lviv's *Ratusha* newspaper wrote, "A philosophical work, full of images, *Raven* intertwines music, folklore, movement, and incredibly beautiful projected images that include live video . . . Lviv doesn't often see the kind of theatrical experiments shown by Virlana Tkacz and her Yara Arts Group. They are definitely worth seeing."

On opening night, Oleh Lysheha sat in the center. Seated next to him was Taras Pastukh, who has written a book on the Kyiv School of Poets and was writing a monograph on Lysheha. After the show, Taras spoke to the audience. He said he felt that the transcendent qualities of the production reflected the transcendental nature of Oleh's work.

The poet Victor Neborak, who had just returned from a major poetry conference, told the audience about how highly Lysheha was now regarded by the major poets of Poland and other East European countries. Somehow, Victor mentioned Shakespeare, so when Oleh got up to speak, he began with "To be or not to be . . ." The audience laughed. Lysheha continued the speech and stunned the entire theatre, not only with his English, but with his memory.

The next morning, I met Oleh for coffee at one of Lviv's wonderful little cafés. We chatted about the production and the translations I had done with Wanda. He asked about my plans for the future. I told him that in a few days I was going to Bishkek,

Kyrgyzstan to start working on a piece about dreams. Oleh shuffled through his papers, the proofs for his new book, and pulled out a few pages. It was a poem called "Dream." He told me he had written it long ago but had never published it. Now, it would be the final poem in a book that was to come out in September. I thanked him, made a copy of the pages, and put them in my pile of papers.

DREAM BRIDGE

AT THE END OF JUNE 2011, I traveled to Kyrgyzstan with Andrew Colteaux. The following morning, Andrew and I started teaching a masterclass at the local Theatre for Young Audiences. Many of the participants were old friends and colleagues.

Kenzhegul Satybaldieva, one the greatest actors I've worked with, created and performed the role of the Kyrgyz mother in *Scythian Stones,* our recent show with Nina Matvienko. She also played the woman warrior in *Janyl.* Together we created *Er Toshtuk,* the humorous show Yara brought to New York in 2009 that was based on the Kyrgyz epic about a young man who falls into the Underworld. Four of the actors in that show were now in our masterclass. Towards the end of each three-hour session, the actors would do improvisations on dreams.

For several years, I have been interested in creating a theatre piece based on dreams. Our dreams can bring to light the mystery that swirls silently in our souls. At night, our brains, freed of their burdens, soar like music. Space turns fluid, as we swim through the universe and through time: into our past and even the future. Dreams become the bridge into our childhood, where we can find answers to lifelong questions or stumble upon new enigmas. We can relive former joys and loves or, once again, experience sharp pain and confusion.

We were developing some interesting material, but the going was slow. I decided we needed a longer text as the framework. As I leafed through my pile of papers one night, I found the Lysheha poem. I realized this was exactly what I needed. I began translating it into English and showed it to Andrew, who agreed. Next morning, I showed it to Kenje, or rather I retold the poem to her, as she doesn't read English or Ukrainian. She too thought it was just what we needed, but asked who was going to do the Kyrgyz translation?

As soon as the question arose, we knew we would have to do it ourselves. We started that night, line by line, out loud—just as I have always worked on translations with Wanda. I have also worked this way with Buryat and Kyrgyz poets on translations of their epics. Four days later, we had our first draft. I showed it to our literary manager and several local poets. They all agreed: it was unusual, but interesting and very good.

We chose eight participants from our masterclass and started working with them on a new Yara show *Dream Bridge,* a theatrical journey into the land of dreams. Together, through a collaborative rehearsal process, we started translating the poetry into theatre. Lysheha's poetry formed the core text of *Dream Bridge,* but no one in our Bishkek cast spoke Ukrainian. Andrew who played the dreamer, spoke English. The rest of the cast played an ensemble of fish that transformed into other characters: the dreamer as a young man, his mother, father, grandmother, his beloved and his friends—all speaking Kyrgyz. The songs in the show were created by Kenje, with music by Nurbek Serkebaev who performed on traditional Kyrgyz instruments.

Dream Bridge also included two scenes from Shakespeare's *A Midsummer Night's Dream,* performed in Kyrgyz. This Shakespeare play is mentioned in the last section of the Lysheha poem. Then one day in rehearsal, Andrew started: "To be or not to be . . . ," imitating Oleh Lysheha's rendition in Lviv. At first, the Kyrgyz actors and I were all on the floor laughing. Then, we were amazed and finally very moved. We decided to include this Shakespearean monologue from *Hamlet* in our show in English.

The workshop production of *Dream Bridge* was performed July 30 - 31, 2011, at the Gallery of Union of Artists of Kyrgyzstan. I created the projections for the show. The lights were designed by

Begaim Turumbekova and the costumes were by Ainura Asanbekova. It was a highly visual and evocative show that was completely accessible to all, no matter what language they spoke.

Kyrgyz poet Roza Mukasheva wrote:

> This show, with its shifting scenes like visions, can help us return to primordial images that seem impossible to experience today as we are overwhelmed by global problems and ever-changing technology. The director is uniquely unrestrained. In her productions, she has allowed us to experience real, primal, and astonishing images that resonate with the secret desires and worries. True colors and natural rhythms exist in her world, supported by the subtle range of tones in the music.

We worked on *Dream Bridge* throughout the year, developing the piece to include Yara actors from New York. Then in the spring, I traveled with Andrew Colteaux, Brian Dolphin, and Christopher Ignacio to Kyiv. There we met our Kyrgyz colleagues, Kenje and Ainura Kachkynbek Kyzy and musician Nurbek Serkebaev. We also included Ukrainian actors Mykola Shkaraban and Vladyslava Havryliuk in the Kyiv version of our show.

While we were rehearsing *Dream Bridge* in Kyiv, I met with Oleh Lysheha and was able to modify the translation we used for performance. I also layered additional texts by Lysheha into the script to amplify the power of the original poems. Oleh related personal memories that inspired the poems. For instance, I discovered why he mentioned Shakespeare in the last section. Lysheha grew up on a river in the foothills of the Carpathians. There was a small bridge over a stream where they played as children, and, as part of a game, they would recite lines from Shakespeare before jumping into the river. Based on this story, Yara redid the scene in *Dream Bridge,* which used fragments of Shakespeare's *A Midsummer Night's Dream.* Lysheha also appreciated our use of the monologue from *Hamlet* that led to the climax of the piece.

We performed our show in Kyiv for the opening of the conference celebrating the one-hundred-twenty-fifth anniversary of Ukrainian director Les Kurbas. Ukraine's most influential paper, *Den,* ran an article on the conference, which featured a photo from Yara's show. The audience included many important theatre artists and scholars from all over the world. Additional performances of *Dream Bridge* at the Pasika Theatre Center were packed with students, experimental theatre-goers, and Yara fans.

One of Yara's newest members, Christopher Ignacio, who is originally from Texas, described his experience of working in Ukraine:

> Through my experience working with actors from other countries, I realized how much we Americans take for granted—like heated rehearsal spaces for one thing! And because the quality of life tends to be easier in the US, our work ethic tends to be somewhat lax as well, at least in comparison with the other actors we worked with. I want to work more like the Kyrgyz and Ukrainian actors, trying everything with full and honest energy until a discovery is made, as opposed to waiting for a director to tell you what to do. They were much more creative, and never complained. I aspire towards that attitude.
>
> I'm also grateful to have worked with Kenzhegul Satybaldieva, a beautiful actress from Kyrgyzstan, who taught me about lightness and the complexities embedded in simple acts. She reminded me of how we tend to forget that theatre is play. I learned all this from her despite our language differences. There was no barrier, and that is what makes me love the theatre and ultimately what Yara strives to accomplish through our work . . . Ukraine was one of the last countries in the world I ever thought I would find myself working in, which is why I'm glad it ended up being one of the first.

In May, the cast traveled to New York, where Kat Yew took over the part Vladislava played in Kyiv. Sean Eden was to take over Mykola Shkaraban's role, but this time could not do so. We had to reassign his lines to others, but this character was sorely missed in the New York production.

On the other hand, the design and its fulfillment grew exponentially in New York. Watoku Ueno's design distilled our workshop ideas to a minimum and then had these ideas visually explode on stage. Ihor Slabicky described the design in detail in his review of the show:

> The plot is quite simple and straightforward—a person falls asleep and dreams. What is told and how it is presented is where the beauty lies in this work. The opening set itself consisted of a white stage floor. To the side was a bed cum bench cum bridge, on which lies the restless Dreamer. Made from old timbers, the curves and arches of this one very solid prop made it seem to always be in motion. When the Dreamer finally did fall asleep, translucent white curtains cascaded down, outlining the stage area on three sides from ceiling to the floor and transforming it into the dream space. These curtains became an integral part of the piece, providing screens for the projections, as well as the surfaces on which the stage lighting was used to great effect.
>
> The dreams themselves consisted of short vignettes—fishing in the river, washing the dishes at home, digging potatoes, visiting his grandmother, performing a fragment of Shakespeare, jumping in the river, and others.
>
> The choreography for this work was utterly amazing. This work has to be one of the most physically demanding pieces that Ms. Tkacz has ever produced. The translucent white screens surrounding the stage on three sides permit the use of video and image projections by Mr. Shraga, which added an extra dimension

to the dreams, making them seem both real and dream-like at the same time. How does a producer present a dream on stage? Ms. Tkacz chose to present the dreams as crystalline reality, the way dreams really do occur in our sleep, leaping from scene to scene, each separate and complete. This was the key to interpreting the dreams described in Lysheha's poems. In the final scenes, when the Dreamer achieved a fitful sleep and the translucent curtains fell to the floor, one was left with the wonderful feeling of having had pleasant dreams, and unlike one's own dreams, remembering them.

—*Ihor Slabicky, The Ukrainian Weekly, July 29, 2012*

LVIV FORUM & MOUNTAIN

IN SEPTEMBER 2011, I was invited to create a presentation for *Translit*—the first International Translation Festival that became a part of the annual Forum of Book Publishers in Lviv. The Forum is both a book market and a literary festival attended by thousands of people. It features over eight-hundred events, with publishers presenting their best books, panelists discussing hot topics, and writers reading their newest texts. For four days the Forum takes over the center of Lviv, including the Potocki Palace.

We called our event "Ukrainian Poetry in Translations: From the Page to the Stage," and it attracted a number of major writers, as well as people interested in translations. Yara's event included a visual aspect, which distinguished it from all the other events. I started my presentation with the question: "What do poems look like when they get translated—both on the page and on the stage?" I showed images of how Yara met visual challenges on the page posed by translations of poems by such contemporary writers as Andriy Bondar and Victor Neborak, or the Futurist Mikhail Semenko.

I continued my presentation by showing the different ways Yara has presented poetry on stage: as readings, songs, and as bilingual performances that intertwine the two languages. We then turned to Yara's theatre pieces. Oleh Lysheha read a section of his poem "Swan," and I showed a video clip from Yara's 2003 production. Oleh then read his prose piece "De Luminis," and I showed photos of Krakow's Archeological Museum, where the piece takes place. Together we read "Song 212" and I showed images of the poem being projected on the new Cooper Union Building as part of the New Ideas Festival.

The following fall, I was invited to create another event for *Translit*. On September 15, 2012, Yara presented "Transforming Ukrainian Poetry into Theatre in New York." This time Oleh Lysheha began by reading his poem "Song 212," and I told the story of how I assumed the poem was about New York because 212 is the city's telephone area code. Then Oleh read sections of his "Raven" in the original, and I showed video clips with those scenes from Yara's *Raven* at La MaMa in 2011. Lysheha also read "Mountain," about a trip to the Carpathian village of Kryvorivnia. This was one of the first works by Lysheha I translated with Wanda Phipps. It was also the reason I chose to record the Koliada in this village in 2003.

During the summer of 2012, I was in Kryvorivnia again, this time working on a new show with the Koliadnyky. We invited Oleh to join us in the mountains and he did. We visited the places he mentioned in his piece: the old house and smithy. The house was still there, but we found no trace of the smithy, which was already overgrown with weeds back in the 1980s.

We did get to sit on a rock on which Franko sat (according to local legend) and take in the special air of Kryvorivnia, a village that drew many Ukrainian writers and scholars at the beginning of the twentieth century. We visited the wonderful little museum in the house where Franko lived, as well as the restored home of Mykhailo Hrushevsky. We saw the plaque on a traditional building near the church that attests to that fact that Lesia Ukrainian slept there. The church itself, built in the 17th century, has seen many remarkable visitors. Kryvorivnia was also the setting for Mykhailo

Kostiubynsky's *Shadows of Forgotten Ancestors,* and in the 1960s Serhiy Parajanov shot many scenes here for his award-winning film based on the novel. The locals take great pride in their history and their traditions. Ethnographers such as Volodymyr Shukhevych, Volodymyr Hnatiuk and Stanislaw Vincenz have flocked here since the 19th century. Even today every winter more than eighty men spend twelve days singing the Koliada winter songs to every "living breath" in their village.

We hoped to work with Oleh Lysheha on a new project called *Mountain* in the village of Kryvorivnia. It would address the presence of the past in our lives, and the importance of turning to the future. We hoped to pose the question of how people who still live in traditional settings can be open to a global world without becoming overwhelmed. We wanted to ask the young villagers how they see themselves in the future. We were hoping Oleh would help us find the words to address the difficult yet essential questions traditional life faces today. We can hear the voices of "children shouting into the heavens." But what are they shouting about?

ADAMO ET DIANA

LYSHEHA WAS VERY SURPRISED to hear that one of the pieces I hoped to translate was his longer prose piece, "Adamo et Diana." I had translated "De Luminis" section for our last Yara Theatre Workshop at Harvard in 1998. During our 2012 Lviv Book Forum event, I once again turned to this text. I had recently been to Krakow and visited the Archeological Museum, where this first section of Lysheha's prose piece takes place. I took many pictures at the museum that had been renovated since Lysheha had described it. The statue of Svito-vyd now had its own separate room and just outside there was a beautiful outdoor courtyard where I could imagine a summer performance. But this performance and my translation of "Adamo et Diana" never transpired. Neither did our collaboration in Kryvorivnia on *Mountain*.

With the protests at the Maidan and the war in Ukraine, Yara projects sent me in a different direction for the next few years. Then one day in December 2014, when I was almost ready to take them up again, I heard the news I couldn't at first comprehend. Oleh Lysheha had passed away.

Parts of this essay were previously published in The Ukrainian Weekly *(June 21, 1998, September 18, 2011 and November 25, 2012), in* Krytyka *March, 2006 and in the events section of* In a Different Light: A Bilingual Anthology of Ukrainian Literature Translated into English by Virlana Tkacz and Wanda Phipps as Performed by Yara Arts Group, *edited by Olha Luchuk. Lviv: Sribne Slovo, 2008*

LETTER FROM OLEH LYSHEHA
TO VIRLANA TKACZ

August 31, 1995

Dear Virlana!

I am glad you liked "Swan." Actually, the "heroes" of my poems—"Fox," "Marten," "Carp," etc.—are beings that are not exactly human. As perhaps you've noticed, "Swan" walks down the road through the forest at night to Hlevakha (where there is a famous psychiatric hospital). I lived there (not in the hospital, of course) after my travels through Europe. Before Europe I was interested in ancient China and its poetry. Maybe there is something in this character from Mallarme or Baudelaire, but perhaps there's more from Chinese tales of shape shifters—so this is a half-man, half-bird spirit. Actually, it's me..

I wouldn't want to insert myself into your translation because I understand how many difficulties you must have encountered. It's a dense forest. I'll mention only a few small details, because overall the translation is accurate. The wire in the shoe is a copper wire used in place of a shoelace.

Later, he is alone on a road that cuts through a forest. Maybe just a few minutes before, that very night, some people from the night train, which stops not far from here, ran down this road. They ran home alone or in groups. This is the setting—a road in a forest at night, a moon, pine trees and their shadows.. He is looking for just *one* cigarette butt—he's not simply smoking some tobacco.

The woman runs with a large bouquet of *pivnyky*—that is: irises. In the summer their exhausted petals, dusted with yellow powder, swing helplessly in the wind. This armful of flowers that hangs down and seems to embrace her. The sleepy hands are the flowers—the irises, or *pivnyky,* as villagers call them. Metaphorically, they become little children, maybe even those not yet born.. At the end—Derhach begs on the trains—that is, he walks through

147

the train cars with a hat and asks for money like a beggar. He does not wait at the train station.

There's one more thing. Have you noticed that at the end of some lines I put two periods, not three? This is important to me because three periods mark the break in thought for longer time in standard punctuation. But two periods suggest a shorter pause, and perhaps are more emotional, not simply punctuation. Every line is a line of the inner monologue that the main character has with himself, remembering some things, forgetting other things and then the lines break off. He is not very old but has lived several lifetimes already. After their careers in the capital, mountains were the refuge of ancient Chinese wisemen-poets.

Virlana, everything I mentioned here are almost insignificant details. Details that are important only to me.. You cannot imagine how interested I would be to see your work on stage. Once I wanted to stage some of the poems myself.. but you beat me to it. I am very pleased that Oleh Drach likes the poem. I do not know him personally—I only saw him from afar in Lublin or Gdansk.. Please send him my greetings. When my book *To Snow and Fire* finally comes out, I will definitely send you a copy. "Swan" is really my most recent work. I have not written anything in several years. In the past few days, I started a grandiose project—an anthology of American poetry. I am collecting, translating, and commenting on the works all by myself. I must finish it in a year. I will include a number of Native American authors.. But I don't seem to be able to write anything of my own. A couple of "private-intimate whirlwinds" have exhausted me to death, and I don't know when I will come to..

I embrace you first of all, then Wanda, Oleh, and the rest..

Oleh Lysheha

YARA ARTS GROUP DOES OLEH LYSHEHA

Theatre Productions

Virtual Souls: With excerpts from "Swan,"was created by Virlana Tkacz with Yara Arts Group and the Buryat National Theatre, music by Genji Ito, designed by Watoku Ueno, movement shaped by Cheng-Chieh Yu, performed at La MaMa Annex in January 1997. Tours included Buryat National Theatre in Ulan Ude, Siberia, Experimental Theatre Festival, Kyiv. The workshop version of *Wayward Wind* was created by Virlana Tkacz with Yara Arts Group, music by Genji Ito and Vladlen Pantaev, designed by Watoku Ueno at La MaMa E.T.C.

Flight of the White Bird: With excerpts from "Swan," created by Virlana Tkacz with Yara Arts Group and the Buryat National Theatre, music by Genji Ito and Erzhena Zhambalov, designed by Watoku Ueno, movement by Cheng-Chieh Yu, performed at La MaMa First Street, April 1998. Premiered at La MaMa Annex, March 1999, Buryat National Theatre, Ulan Ude Siberia, as well as the cultural centers of Aginskoye, Tsagaan Chelutay, Kunkur, Tokchin, and Alkhanay in August 1998.

Swan: Created with Yara artists on the basis of the poem by Oleh Lysheha, directed by Virlana Tkacz, with music by Paul Brantley, set, costumes and lights designed by Watoku Ueno, video by Andrea Odezynska. Premiered at La MaMa E.T.C. June 2003. Also presented at Lowell Hall, Harvard University July 2003.

Raven: Based on Oleh Lysheha's poem, created by Virlana Tkacz and Yara Arts Group with Ukrainian artists. Electronic music by Alla Zahaykevych, songs by Aurelia Shrenker and Eva Salina Primack. Ash/ AE, and Julian Kytasty. Light design by Zhenya Kopiov, projections by Waldemart Klyuzko and Mikhail Shraga, costumes by Keiko Obremski. Nominated for New York Innovative Theatre Award for Innovative Design. Performed at La MaMa ETC, April 2011. Workshop Pasika Theatre Center, Kyiv, March 2011. Toured Pasika Theatre Center, Kyiv, June 2011 and Les Kurbas Theatre, Lviv, June 2011.

Dream Bridge: Based on Oleh Lysheha's poem "Dream," created by Virlana Tkacz with Yara Arts Group and Kyrgyz artists. Music by Alla Zahaykevych and Nurbek Serkebaev, with design by Watoku Ueno, costumes by Ainura Asanbekova, projections by Mikhail Shraga and

Waldemart Klyuzko. Workshopped at Union of Artists of Kyrgyzstan, Bishkek, July 2011, at Pasika Theatre in March 2012, at Les Kurbas Theatre Center, Kyiv, March 2012. Premiered at La MaMa ETC in April 2012.

Harvard Theatre Workshops

July 1991: *Radio Eternity Ukrainian Poetry from the 1920s and the 1990s* featuring "Mountain" by Oleh Lysheha, read by Yuri Shevchuk.

July 1992: *Heart Pic(k)s: 19ᵗʰ and 20ᵗʰ Century Ukrainian Love Poetry* included excerpts from "Friend Li Po, Brother Tu Fu," read by Natalia Pylypiuk.

July 1995: *Oceanic Consciousness: Growing Fangs, Tails, and Wings,* featured "Swan" by Oleh Lysheha, performed in Ukrainian by Oleh Drach.

July 1997: *Seven Veils: A Theatrical Presentation of Seven Very Contemporary Ukrainian Poets* included "Museum" and an excerpt from "Swan" by Oleh Lysheha, music by Genji Ito.

July 1998: *Messenger: A Theatre Presentation of Contemporary Ukrainian Poetry* featured "De Luminis," an excerpt from *Adamo et Diana* by Oleh Lysheha.

Other Yara Events with Oleh Lysheha's Poetry

May 1992: A bilingual reading of Oleh Lysheha's "Song 212" at the Ukrainian Institute of America, New York.

April 1993: A bilingual reading of Oleh Lysheha's "Song 2" and "Song 212" at La MaMa Galleria, New York.

October 1996: An excerpt from Oleh Lysheha's "Swan" at The Washington Group Conference.

May 1997: A bilingual reading of Oleh Lysheha's "Bear" at the Ukrainian Institute of America, New York.

April 1998: *A Celebration of the Poetry of Oleh Lysheha*: Oleh Lysheha read his work in Ukrainian, while Yara actors read English translations of his work at the Mayana Gallery, New York.

January 1999: *InVerse / Poetry: Installations and Performances* included readings of Oleh Lysheha's poems and the exhibition of *Song 2,* with installation by Petro Hrycyk and *Mountain* installation by Watoku Ueno inspired by Lysheha's poems, at the Ukrainian Institute of America, New York.

October 2001: Yara actors perform poetry from *A Hundred Years of Youth,* including Oleh Lysheha's "Song 212" and an excerpt from "Swan" performed by Meredith Wright at the Tompkins Square Branch, New York Public Library.

January 2002: Meredith Wright sang "The Swan Appears" from Oleh Lysheha's "Swan" at *Cold Change: The Alternative New Year's Day Spoken Word / Performance* at the Knitting Factory, New York.

January 2003: *kolo nas 4* presents oleh lysheha *talk on poetry* and the presentation of his new book, *To Snow and Fire* at the Kyiv Mohyla Academy, Kyiv.

July 2003: Performances of Oleh Lysheha's "Song 212" and an excerpt from "Swan." Soyuzivka, Kerhonkson, New York.

October 2003: *kolo nas 5* presents taras prokhasko and oleh lysheha present 'another format' book series at the RA Gallery, Kyiv.

May 2004: A reading of Oleh Lysheha's poetry in translation at the presentation of *Poetry International Web—Ukraine* by the Embassy of the Netherlands at the British Council, Kyiv.

September 2005: *Yara Celebrates 15 Years* included excerpts from Oleh Lysheha's "Swan" at La MaMa Annex, New York.

November 2005: *InVerse* included excerpts from Oleh Lysheha's "Swan" at Dutchess Community College, Poughkeepsie, NY.

January 2008: *In a Different Light* was an exhibit of installations, performances, and food inspired by Ukrainian poetry. Two menu items served were inspired by Oleh Lysheha poems, at the Ukrainian Institute of America, New York.

June 2008: *In a Different Light,* a poetry event celebrating the publication of the bilingual anthology of poetry used in Yara Arts Group theatre pieces from 1990 through 2002. Readers included Oleh Lysheha, at the Potocki Palace, Lviv.

May 2011: *A White Wing Brushing the Building: Poetry in NYC Communities*, a bilingual performance of poetry by Oleh Lysheha at the Bowery Arts and Science, The Cooper Union, New York.

September 2011: *Ukrainian Poetry in Translations: From the Page to the Stage* bilingual presentation, including Oleh Lysheha's "Swan," "De Luminis," and "Song 212" at the Voskresinnia Theatre, Lviv.

September 2012: *Yara Arts Group: Transforming Ukrainian Poetry into Theatre* presentation by Virlana Tkacz. Bilingual readings of poetry by actors and poets, including Oleh Lysheha's "Song 212" and "Mountains," plus video excerpts from "Swan" and "Raven" at the Voskresinnia Theatre, Lviv.

January 2015: *Yara at 25: Looking Back/Moving Forward* exhibition recalling Yara's productions, including a blue suitcase with a photo and excerpt from Oleh Lysheha's "Raven" at the Ukrainian Museum, New York.

January 2015: *Yara at 25 Live* event included Meredith Wright singing "The Swan Appears" section of Lysheha's 'Swan' at the Ukrainian Museum, New York.

February 2016: *Yara Arts Group: Looking Back / Moving Forward* exhibition at the Museum of Theatre, Music, and Cinema, Kyiv.

YARA'S VIRTUAL EVENTS ABOUT OLEH LYSHEHA

June 2020: *Yara's Theatre Projects*: *Poetry as Theatre:* Oleh Lysheha's "Swan" with Virlana Tkacz and Yara artists who created and performed the theatre pieces with the poem in 1996, 1999, and 2003. Virtual event with over 1,400 views.

October 2020: *Yara's Theatre Projects: Poetry as Theatre:* Oleh Lysheha's "Raven" with Virlana Tkacz and Yara artists who created and performed the theatre piece in 2011 in Kyiv, La MaMa, and Lviv. Virtual event with over 1,400 views.

October 2020: *Oleh Lysheha: Poetry in Theatre:* Media talk by Virlana Tkacz on Yara's Theatre Productions of *Swan, Raven,* and *Dream Bridge.* Virtual event in Ukrainian, live streamed and recorded.

PUBLISHED TRANSLATIONS BY VIRLANA TKACZ & WANDA PHIPPS OF OLEH LYSHEHA'S POETRY

Books:

In a Different Light: A Bilingual Anthology of Ukrainian Literature Translated into English by Virlana Tkacz and Wanda Phipps as Performed by Yara Arts Group, edited by Olha Luchuk. Lviv: Sribne Slovo, 2008. Includes Oleh Lysheha's "Bear," "The Mountain," "On Learning New Party Hymns," "Song 2," "Song 212," and "Swan."

A Hundred Years of Youth: A Bilingual Anthology of 20th Century Ukrainian Poetry, edited by Olha Luchuk and Michael Naydan, (Litopys: Lviv, 2000), includes Lysheha's "Song 212."

Ten Years of Poetry from the Yara Theatre Workshops at Harvard (1997) includes: Lysheha's "Museum" excerpt from "Swan."

Journals:

Oleh Lysheha's excerpts from "Raven," *Loch Raven Review*, Vol 14 No 2, 2018. https://thelochravenreview.net/ten-ukrainian-poets.

Oleh Lysheha's "Song 212" and "Song 2," *Visions International* 52, (Fall 1996).

Oleh Lysheha's "On Learning New Party Hymns," *Index on Censorship* (March 1993).

Websites:

Lysheha's poems "Horse," "Song 212," "Song 2," and "Bear": *https://www.poetryinternational.org/pi/poet/5525/Oleh-Lysheha/en/tile: Poetry International Web—Ukraine*

Yara Arts Group: www.*yaraartsgroup.net*

THE AUTHOR

OLEH LYSHEHA was born on October 30, 1949 in Tysmenytsia, near the Carpathian Mountains in Ukraine. He studied foreign languages and was expelled from Lviv University during a purge in 1972 for his interest in contemporary American poetry. He was drafted and sent to do military duty in Siberia and in the Buryat Republic. There he found his lifelong interest in Asian and indigenous cultures. When he returned to Ukraine, Lysheha was isolated from official Soviet literary activities and was not published throughout the 1970s and 1980s. His first collection of poetry, *The Great Bridge,* published in 1989, was like nothing else printed in the official sources. In 1994 *Suchasnist* journal published a cycle of his longer poems. He also published his poems and prose pieces in the journal *Svito-vyd.* He was a Fulbright Scholar and writer-in-residence at Pennsylvania State University from 1997 to 1998. *The Selected Poems of Oleh Lysheha* in English translations by the author and James Brasfield was published in 1999 by the Ukrainian Institute at Harvard and was awarded the PEN Translation Prize.

In 2002 Lysheha published his collection *To Snow and Fire.* The 2012 edition of *The Great Bridge* included Lysheha's newer work. In 2014, Ivan Malkovych published *Winter in Tysnmenytsia; Selected Poems by Oleh Lysheha* in A-Ba-Ba-Ha-La-Ma-Ha's prestigious *Ukrainian Poetry Anthology Series.* Oleh Lysheha died in Kyiv on December 17, 2014.

Lysheha's poetry has been incorporated into a number of theatre pieces created by the Yara Arts Group, including *Virtual Souls* and *Flight of the White Bird.* In 2003 Yara staged his poem *Swan* and in 2011 *Raven,* which was nominated for a New York Innovative Theatre award for design. In 2013 Yara created *Dream Bridge,* which included Lysheha's earliest poems.

THE TRANSLATORS

VIRLANA TKACZ and WANDA PHIPPS have received the Agni Poetry Translation Prize, the National Theatre Translation Fund Award, and thirteen translation grants from the New York State Council on the Arts. *What We Live For / What We Die For: Selected Poems by Serhiy Zhadan*, with translations by Virlana Tkacz and Wanda Phipps, was published by Yale University Press in 2019. Their translations have also appeared in many literary journals and anthologies, and are integral to the theatre pieces created by Yara Arts Group.

VIRLANA TKACZ heads the Yara Arts Group and has directed almost forty original shows at La MaMa Theatre in New York, as well as in Kyiv, Lviv, Kharkiv, Bishkek, Ulaanbaatar, and Ulan Ude. She has received an NEA Poetry Translation Fellowship for her translations with Wanda Phipps.

WANDA PHIPPS is the author of the books *Mind Honey, Field of Wanting: Poems of Desire,* and *Wake-Up Calls: 66 Morning Poems*. She received a New York Foundation for the Arts Poetry Fellowship. Her poems have appeared in over one-hundred literary magazines and numerous anthologies.